JOHN HEARTFIELD:
ART AND MASS MEDIA

Douglas Kahn

TANAM PRESS NEW YORK 1985

D1513359

TANAM PRESS GRATEFULLY ACKNOWLEDGES SUPPORT FROM
THE NEW YORK STATE COUNCIL ON THE ARTS
LITERATURE PROGRAM

FOR SAM AND RUBY

CONTENTS

INTRODUCTION

Kurt Rosenfeld, Minister of Justice of Prussia during the Weimar Republic, had "a painting in his office by Daumier called *Justice Violated by a Judge*, which had hung almost unnoticed on his walls for a year. [In 1933 it...] was reported as treasonable and caused his hurried departure from Germany."[1] John Heartfield had to abandon an original Daumier graphic in his Berlin apartment during his own hurried departure from Hitler's Germany. On Easter 1933, two months after Hitler assumed power, the 41-year-old Heartfield discreetly returned to check his apartment after having stayed with friends for some time. As it turned out he was just a few steps ahead of the SS. As they came up the stairs he left through a window and, enabled by his small size, hid behind a barber's sign before making his way to Prague to join those already in exile. There he persisted in being a consummate "pain in the ass". A 1936 Nazi publication *World Communism* contained a full-page photograph showing him dressed as a stern, black-robed German judge violating justice by holding an imbalanced scales of justice in full view. When the Nazis pressed Czechoslovakia for his extradition Heartfield left for London, staying there from 1938 to 1950. In 1942 he wrote an article on Daumier for the *Journal of the League for Free German Culture* (London). Wondering about his Daumier graphic he asks, "Perhaps it is in the possession of the burglars?"

Over forty years have passed; it now has to be asked where's the Heartfield? A number of commentators have characterized Heartfield as being to the 20th century what Daumier was to the 19th. Yet in the English speaking nations he has received little attention. The neglect is almost as famous as he is. Lesser figures have enjoyed minute scholarly treatments and oversized coffee table editions. The absence of scholarly attention in English is itself in need of scholarly attention. The weight of his work, however, will probably remain too heavy for the American coffee table, although it is possible for him to be belatedly recuperated in the manner, say, Daumier was subsequently recuperated by the Nazis in the 30s.

Heartfield was responsible for the development of political photomontage. The development occurred in a synthesis of two fertile phenomena in the early-20th century, the Bohemian avant-garde and the Marxist-Leninist vanguard, and appeared weekly in another potent phenomenon, the mass media, during the period of its historical consolidation. It was a cultural practice political at all points of its conception, a politics of form as well as content, one which structured in the mass media processes of literacy as well as distribution, and it is still of great relevance for cultural practitioners today. He is one of the few major political artists of this century and he is the first artist (outside film) of the mass media—and, to date, the most significant.

To translate what he did into present-day North Americanese, think of photomontage as the editorial cartooning found in the daily paper. But instead of being drawn it is constructed from cut-up photographs, many of which have appeared in other newspapers or look as though they could have appeared there. Instead of a daily newspaper it is a large format photo weekly akin to *Life* magazine. Technically, his photomontages are high quality, copper tint in color, as is the entire magazine, and occupy a full or double-page spread, at times the front or back cover. Because the photojournalistic images are familiar they look, at first glance, as if the well-known individuals depicted were going through some very odd, usually self-incriminating motions, caught in the act just below the static surface of photographic appearance, where deals are struck, meaning unfolds and actual history resides.

His photomontages appeared in a communist publication known by the initials A-I-Z, short for Arbeiter Illustriete Zeitung or

Workers Illustrated Paper. Of the famous illustrated magazines during the Weimar Republic it held a competitive position boasting the third, at times second, largest circulation. These magazines were the vehicles for the "new photography," the birth of modern photojournalism, when a daily ration of photography was still greeted with fascination, enthusiasm and a confidence that what was depicted had a bear hug on reality. They enjoyed this status in the field of representation because they themselves represented the most advanced form of mass media. In this respect, to truly translate Heartfield into the present, his work would have to appear regularly on one of the major television networks delivering anti-capitalist content utilizing media-familiar individuals wrenched from their normal context. The form of his work, whatever form it would take, would itself be a critique of formal conventions of the delivery of meaning on the two other TV networks, and would critique them in such a way as to be residual, i.e., when you watched the other networks his critique would be invoked whenever certain individuals, messages or programming conventions appeared. This ideally would set up a motion running from a general skepticism to an informed critique. And, as with the large working class movement during the Weimar Republic, the criticality would take place in a context of organized political opposition. The result would be that the violence of the U.S. which festers daily below the static surfaces of mass mediated appearance and which breaks skin the more it is globalized would be disclosed and dissected with regularity in a widely disseminated and popularly embraced cultural form.

This book arose out of my own activities as an artist. When I first encountered Heartfield's work I had already been doing audio/radio work which shared features with his involvement in photomontage. Insight gained from an investigation into his work meant insight into aspects of my own, and vice versa. The sheer personal functionality of this investigation was momentum enough to move past the dearth of information on Heartfield to a point where I might be able to contribute to its break-up.

My concern, however, has never been solely to fill in the void of information. There has never been interest in filing for the adoption papers of a dead man. The motivating force has instead been a desire to use a discussion of Heartfield as an occasion to address and pose issues for present day oppositional cultural practice.

The process of generalization with which I related his work to my own belongs to a notion of cultural practice released from the strictures of specific media and disciplines. Such a notion is inherent in his work, a highly integrated instance of a number of socio-cultural influences and practices: photography, mass print media, journalism, avant-garde art, commercial art, working class political organization and revolutionary politics. If his work could be reduced descriptively to a specific practice it would be revolutionary working class parodic photojournalism.

The development of his work was an accumulative coordination of various practices, maturing in 1930 then cut short upon exile. This period stretched the entire length of the Weimar Republic, overhanging a little on either end. On the earlier end was the middle of World War I. Heartfield, then with his given name Herzfeld, had come to Berlin in 1913, the year before the war, and was soon joined by his brother Wieland. Both entered the Berlin Bohemian circles suffused with a ripened expressionism. Heartfield brought with him a dual background in fine and commercial art, the younger Wieland aspirations toward poetry and writing. Heartfield was able to avoid combat and instead collaborated with George Grosz in his first acts of politicizing culture, which took the form of packages and primitive photomontages sent to the front, as well as other activities.

Before the war was over the Russian Revolution of October 1917 redirected the anti-war political tendencies among the dissent of the Bohemians in Germany by presenting the possibility for the rewriting of more than artistic and aesthetic history. In this light Germany's approaching defeat took on added proportions, strengthening the anti-militarism for sure, while fueling the audacity and irreverence of those around Heartfield who had been eager for the day for some time already. This is the context in which his proto-dada graphics for Wieland's journal *Neue Jugend* were fostered—a cubistic effluence given political confidence.

By the time the war ended, dissent which had been endemic became epidemic resulting in the so-called November Revolution of 1918. Unlike the communist revolution one year and one

4

month before, the November Revolution ushered in a social democratic Weimar Republic, a liberal bourgeois regime maintained through its constitution and the Social Democratic Party's (SPD) control of coalition governments, i.e., up to the Brüning government. The suppression and direct repression of opposition began immediately, the conflict continuing without respite until 1924. From Heartfield's vantage point, the social democratic course of action was betrayal from the very beginning since the SPD had assumed remedial control over a nation they had helped to lead off to war. This betrayal took on an historical conception once Heartfield had joined, on the day of its founding, the German Communist Party (KPD). It was also confirmed through the early brutality of the SPD and through the survival and growth of the Russian Revolution.

All this was in place by the time dada proper came about. Berlin Dada is known as the political one among its namesakes. What may be known but not stated is that a number of its central members were also members of the KPD (this is often circumvented by failing to mention Heartfield's central role in Berlin Dada). Heartfield's participation in dada buttressed his recent fusion of avantgarde art and vanguard politics. The intermittance of occasions to act presented by Berlin Dada was relieved by the protracted work he found within the publishing house, an outgrowth of the earlier publishing efforts of his brother, Malik Verlag. Heartfield's commercial work designing books and bookcovers for Malik Verlag served to place a governor upon the dadaist formal tendencies toward an unfettered collage effluence, simplifying and centralizing his imagery. He also worked in theater set design, most importantly with the Communist director Erwin Piscator. The paring down exerted upon Heartfield's work by the commercialist mandates of Malik was reversed during his work with Piscator where a practical model for the rationalistic saturation of a single moment or space with elements normally belonging to other media or disciplines was introduced. From this came the simultaneous presence in Heartfield's mature work of photography, journalistic format of header, caption and text, commentary, poetry, drawing and painting, etc. Work with Piscator also introduced an applied socio-aesthetic of documentary and journalism where notions of history of the past and of the moment could be represented.

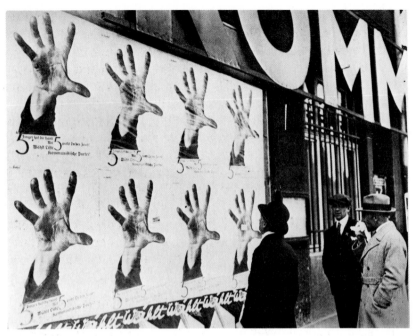

Poster for 20 May 1928 Election: "The hand has 5 fingers / with 5 you seize the enemy! / Vote list 5 / Communist Party!"

Both Heartfield and Piscator were on the ground floor of Weimar's left modernism movement, a diverse cultural phenomenon whose best known participant was Bertolt Brecht. It began with a rejection of expressionism, nationalism and national culture, and social democracy, plus an embracing of events in Russia. It rejected expressionism's mysticism and subjectivism while politicizing its Promethean objectives and personal exuberance. It therefore had no difficulty in skirting the scientist and detached surface inspections characteristic of Neue Sachlichkeit (New matter-of-factness), the major artistic wave hitting Weimar in the mid-20s.

Through the latter half of the 20s the left modernists moved closer to the working class movement, joining in on its immense social and cultural life. Heartfield, as many other artists and intellectuals, effected this allegiance through the KPD, working in the propaganda-agitation section (which would probably be called "public relations", maybe "social relations", today). The contact with party leadership and activists made his work more purposive, directing it toward the central political concerns of the day. This could be called "topicality" if it were not for the historicization and epochal considerations brought to events by the brand of orthodox Marxism practiced by the KPD, not to mention the persistent transcendent tug from Heartfield's fine arts background.

The latter half of the 20s also saw an unprecedented expansion, an explosion of the mass media in Weimar. The individual most responsible for creating an oppositional and communist presence within this phenomenon was Willi Münzenberg. His efforts in this respect greatly aided the alliance of the left modernists and the working class movement, and vice versa. He was at the crucial pivotal point of the politicized avant-garde and mass (class) media and culture. Hans Magnus Enzensberger mentioned him parenthetically in his well known article from the early 1970s "Constituents of a Theory of the Media."[2]

> The inadequate understanding which Marxists have shown of the media and the questionable use they have made of them has produced a vacuum in Western industrialized countries into which a stream of non-Marxist hypotheses and practices has consequently flowed. From the Cabaret Voltaire to Andy Warhol's Factory, from the silent film comedians to the Beatles, from the first comic strip artists to the present managers of the Underground, the apolitical have made much more radical progress in dealing with the media than any grouping of the Left. (Exception - Münzenberg.)

He shares with Heartfield a high degree of integration of, and a great deal of mobility around, a range of socio-cultural practices (and he shares a similar degree of present day neglect). It's been said Heartfield implemented a Brechtian aesthetic; it would be more accurate to say Münzenbergian.

As the KPD grew in strength with the approaching capitalist crisis of the Great Depression, Heartfield came into orbit around the institutional and organizational brainchildren of Münzenberg, starting with Neue Deutscher Verlag (NDV) which published the successful collaboration between Heartfield and the satirist Kurt Tucholsky, *Deutschland, Deutschland über alles*. Most decisively, and the point which marks the full integration of Heartfield's practice as well as his maturity in other respects, was his tenure with NDV's A-I-Z where his photomontages began regularly appearing

Exhibition in Prague

in 1930. He had previously produced photomontages in manner of appearance with those in A-I-Z but only at this point did they operate at a societal level.

For taking a relatively long time to reach this highest point in his cultural practice (1916-30), it was unfortunately short-lived due to exile in 1933. Exile severely disintegrated the complex of practices which afforded him social centrality in late-Weimar. The media marginalization which had just been conquered took effect again now that A-I-Z was stationed in Prague. Most obviously, the assured weekly circulation fell from around 200,000 to about 12,000 and those mostly outside Gemany. Heartfield joined the staff in Prague, the German opposition parties' national capital in exile, and continued to produce photomontages for the pages of A-I-Z through its incarnations until its demise in the late-30s. Some of his most powerful photomontages were produced during this his most prolific photomontage period, but they occurred in wildly divergent social settings characterized by progressive deterioration, a fact rarely acknowledged in the many short essays on

Heartfield which implicitly see his output as an uninterrupted sequence. The deterioration began with his relationship to the domestic German population for with his flight came an irreparable distancing from the working class in whose name he had worked and continued to work. He grew more and more absent from concrete reception of and vernacular resistance to the mass media by individuals in Germany and was forced to limit himself to German speaking regions in other nations and to the exile community and its supporters. It would have been much more devastating had he not been an internationalist, as was demonstrated by his photomontages during the Spanish Civil War. However, his constituencies became more distant as the Nazis extended their influence, consentually and otherwise.

The process of deterioration was exacerbated by transformations within mass media as a whole. At the very beginning of exile Heartfield produced nearly a dozen photomontages on the Reichstag fire (which provided the pretext for outlawing the KPD and for a general wave of repression) and the show trial which followed. The photomontages appeared in A-I-Z, on postcards, and in the internationally distributed *Brown Books of Nazi Terror*, another project organized by Münzenberg as were the international tribunals in Paris and London where witnesses who could not testify in Germany were heard. The campaign was a large success on the map of world opinion undercutting the anti-communist display of the trial and introducing to the world the hair-trigger brutality of the new regime.

This early success unfortunately would be the only one of such magnitude inflicted by the communists-in-exile upon the Third Reich. It was, afterall, a campaign that could still be waged in print. In Germany the Nazi "coordination" of press and spectacle took place with the rise of broadcast media which superceded the photographic print media by carrying the visceralities of individual speech and disembodied community. Internationally, this culminated with the next major Nazi show trial, the 1936 Berlin Olympiad, a largely successful legitimating spectacle. Although Heartfield produced some very powerful photomontages for the occasion they had to ultimately contend with a global broadcast system of which the Director of NBC in the United States had said, "the work done by the Reichsrudfunk remains without precedent in the history of broadcasting."

9

With the photomontages themselves, exile introduced, beginning immediately with the Reichstag fire trial series, a pedagogical element which had been previously edged out by the hot house polemical assertions of late-Weimar. It was a teaching which usually took the form of informing those outside Germany of events within. This pedagogy was still informed by a perception of the Nazis as being a direct expression of moribund capitalism, an instrumentality of the bourgeoisie. The Popular Front policy of the mid-30s, where a communist distinction between "repressive and non-repressive bourgeoisies" allowed them to enter a broad alliance against fascism and Naziism, took away from Heartfield the bourgeois class object of his vituperation as well as the basis of his theoretical scenario. All around him toleration and trepidation were installed; the certainty of communist rhetoric was replaced by bourgeois democratic demagogics of "freedom" and "democracy"; A-I-Z became VI—*Volks Illustriete* i.e., the workers had become people. Backed up against this mist of liberal humanism Heartfield's work suffered and never really recovered. Of course, all objects of his hate were removed upon the Hitler-Stalin pact.

He left Prague for Longon in 1939 as the Nazis pressed for extradition. VI left for Paris where it sputtered out after a few issues. From this point on he would create very few new photomontages. He did recycle older ones including a photomontage originally appearing in August 1932 showing Hitler in Kaiser Wilhelm II garb. It showed up on the cover of *Picture Post* a matter of days away from Germany's invasion of Poland. England went on war footing where, all of a sudden, everyone was an anti-fascist. Heartfield was interred but released after MP protest, making his way in England working in book design and remaining politically active in the community. He returned to East Germany until 1950 where he joined Wieland, worked with Brecht's Berlin Ensemble and generally became a venerated artist. He had a number of retrospective exhibitions and recycled some more photomontages to adapt to liberation struggles in Africa, nuclear armaments and the Vietnam War. He also worked with Wieland during the early 60s to produce the monograph *John Heartfield: Leben und Werke*. However, he never got back into a critical practice within the media; the role of Münzenberg, who had fallen out of state grace, in making Heartfield's earlier practice possible did not receive mention in the monograph. Heartfield died in 1968.

The harsh consequences of exile have to be qualified by the fact that Heartfield continued working, at times at an accelerated pace, in conditions which had demobilized other artists, intellectuals and activists. Although this experience is highly relevant to those today who are exiled, it is an exceptional case for citizens of bourgeois democracies. For this reason, this book is limited to the time frame of the Weimar period.

I begin with a quick excursion from Heartfield's output during WWI to the single work chosen to represent his mature work of late-Weimar, the "Tiger montage," proceeding in an impressionistic chronology which is interrupted by purely interpretive passages. Heartfield's progression from privatized to socialized cultural practice is followed i.e., from his anti-war actions addressing single individuals to his late-Weimar photomontages reaching millions. The fields of subject matter change accordingly, progressing from the biographically centered to broad societal considerations. The formation of the basic components of his practice, in the personages of Herzfelde, Piscator and Münzenberg, and the institutions with which they were associated, is given in broad outline. The excursion builds up background to the inspection of the Tiger montage as well as presenting background tied to points elsewhere outside this book.

There are reasons why I have selected only one photomontage for analysis and why the Tiger montage in particular, i.e., apart from the fact that if a number of photomontages were subjected to adequate dissection a delayed tome would be in the offing. For Heartfield or any other artist who refuses to fancy their work as arising and rising in a transcendent aesthetic sphere, who instead work toward radical and revolutionary social transformation, they are necessarily immersed within a thick and constantly changing density of decision where even the seemingly insignificant detail resonates with the historical. By using the example of a relatively stationary historical moment (stationary, i.e., when compared to the history of the present) a glancing model of complexity, an approximation of this density of decision can be posed. Suggesting such a model has to be distinguished from conventional historical interpretation in two ways, both disposed toward actual artistic production: a familiarity is sought past the point of representing *what was* to proposing *what could have been* and, consequently, an empathy for the general goals of the work is required, destroying any pretense toward detachment.

Reasons for the choice of the Tiger montage in particular are given at the beginning of that chapter. Another motivation is the desire to dislodge the character of recent attention given Heartfield from the left. In reaction to what is correctly seen as a systemic if not systematic neglect there has been an open-armed uncritical embrace, an ironic occurrence considering that the feature most people find compelling about his work is its criticality. Heartfield, however, regularly suspended his own critical faculties. Excluded from his criticism (but at times invoked for blanket exhortation) were Stalin, the workings of the Comintern, Thälmann, the KPD and the German working class.*

In other words, he was what was known as a "100%-er." He did not stray from the Communists' disastrous analyses, policies and actions toward social democracy, Naziism and fascism, and revolution. A recent film produced in West Berlin which has played in the U.S. promotes Heartfield as an "anti-fascist" in the spirit of the mid-30s Popular Front, while no mention is made that he and the Communists included the Social Democrats among the fascists, elevating them over the Nazis in a hierarchy of fascism and doing so at a very consequential historical moment. The Tiger montage belongs to this moment.

The last chapter "Montage, Mimikry" breaks out of the singular focus and historical localization of the previous chapter. It is concerned instead with situating the general features of Heartfield's work among comparable practices both contemporary with his own and from other times. From an expanded field of "montage" a distinction is made which allows the placement of Heartfield in more select montage company. This distinction simply isolates

---

*(exception: "Hurrah, the butter is finished! Goering in his Hamburg speech: 'Iron always makes the Reich strong, butter and schmalz only make the people fat.'" —depicted an acquiescent family in a patriarchal scene of which neither the working class nor communists were immune. . . but this photomontage, as with nearly all produced in exile, remains incomplete not having rubbed against the daily life of the Germans in Germany).

cultural work which uses "previously cultured" material as raw material. For example, instead of shooting photos, readily recognizable "pre-shot" images are used; instead of writing from observation, inspiration or industry, the result of the process once it has achieved a socially discursive existence forms the jumping off point. It is a cultural production run through the mill once again: squared. As such, it deserves consideration consistent with its odd autonomy, with all the disadvantages and advantages.

For Heartfield, raw material by and large meant photojournalism, pulling it from its place in the bourgeois press, reworking it and returning it almost full circle (350 degrees) to a competitive position. During the same time there existed a similar practice with the genre of compilation films. For this genre's premier practitioner, the Russian filmmaker Esfir Shub, and other practitioners throughout Europe, raw material meant old and foreign films, a preference that had once been dictated by necessity. In prior discussions of Heartfield, cinematic comparisons with Sergei Eisenstein (who Shub taught how to edit) have held sway despite the fact his montage was primarily a mode of artistic organization having no special relation to the origin of what was being organized.

This specification within montage opens up a comparison with another area of cultural activity, *mimikry*. Mimikry is used here to mean a tactical mimesis, tactics which can adapt and have been adapted to political strategies of any coloration. Its oppositional usage is a specific instance of parody (so specific it confuses the issue to call it parody) where the person who is the object of the parody participates. One of the purposes of the emphasis on mimikry is to take the traffic in verisimilitudes out of the sole possession of photo and film talk and into a discussion of a more generalized notion of culture where politics is not as easily excluded. It is also used as a vehicle for a translation of Heartfield's practice into the present: a number of instances of recent mimikry are presented. Finally, it is used as access to the phenomenon of simulation, the context in which any mimikry will occur in the not-too-distant future.

The preconditions for an oppositional cultural practice on a level of social centrality achieved by Heartfield do not presently exist in the U.S. There would have to be a radical democratization within the mass media apparatus for the regular appearance of systemic critique, and this democratization would necessarily be coupled with a larger activitist phenomenon. However, this fact cannot be allowed to rationalize inactivity for reason of nostalgia or erotic fantasy of a political body. Heartfield's relevance must be entertained as actions within spheres of less social centrality, within local and regional settings, or as intermittent incursions on a mass level. Additionally, they will be contained almost entirely, as examples of recent mimikry cited in the last chapter show, to a patently oppositional practice i.e., concentrated on the negation of the mode and substance of oppressions and oppressors. However, present-day affirmative practices, i.e., those which affirm the process of collective empowerment of subjugated social groups and the regeneration of repressed liberatory potentialities, necessarily need to maintain a cognizance of the influence that mass media literacy has extended to every corner of daily life.

The oppositional importance, especially of mimikry, becomes greater when it is seen as one type of interdiction to the future institution of *actual* (not to be confused with the recent recurrence of metaphorical and philosophical usages) simulation, where all the little verisimilitudinal machinations which transport oppositional instances of mimikry so effectively remain undisclosed as such and move toward the frayed oppressive ends this techno-naturalism promises.

Along with the significances for immediate opposition, there are those which are more formative, expansive and sublime. These are to be accessed through the combinatory processes at the heart of Heartfield's artistic method as well as through an imperative for the historicization of the miniscule, that extant distance requiring a point of elevated imagination for its triangulation. It is the elaboration of these which provides the vitalization of a contemporary practice and keeps alive fragments worthy of reclamation.

All in all, Heartfield's work demonstrates two major criteria for oppositional cultural practice: it encourages further opposition and it seeks to destroy itself as an historical necessity (by the destruction of what it opposes). The former is a proliferation to hasten the latter i.e., his work directs an influence toward its own obsolesence. As Heartfield said during the early-60s, "Unfortunately, many of these works from earlier times are still timely. However, I am full of good hope that the struggle of humanity for the preservation of freedom will bring their timeliness to an end in the not too distant future."

In pointing out the neglect Heartfield has suffered I do not wish to devalue the work that has occurred. Of note in English is the writing of Beth Irwin Lewis whose book on Grosz contains valuable information on Heartfield and the Weimar period besides being the best work available on Grosz. Her catalogue *Grosz/Heartfield: The Artist as Social Critic* accompanied the first U.S. exhibition of Heartfield's work since the 1938 Photo League exhibition. This catalogue, along with Universe Book's *John Heartfield: Photomontages of the Nazi Period* should be referred to for a greater number of reproductions than we were able to provide here. See also the 1984 catalogue from the Goethe Institute in New York City *Malik Verlag: 1916-1947*, by James Fraser and Steven Heller.

In the U.S., incomplete sets of A-I-Z are to be found at the Fine Arts Museum-Houston, the Eastman House in Rochester and the Center for Research Library in Chicago. I would like to thank Anne Tucker at the Fine Arts Museum for her assistance. Microfilm of various years of A-I-Z is also available in the United States. The Polytechnic of Central London, Staatsbibliothek Werkbund Archiv in West Berlin, and the Heartfield Archiv in East Berlin are sources in Europe. The photographs in this book reproduced through the kind cooperation of the Heartfield Archiv, The Museum of Fine Arts-Houston, the Bundesarchiv-Koblenz and the The Library of the University of Washington.

In German, Herzfelde's monograph on his brother remains the best source of reproductions (although some differ from the way they appeared originally in A-I-Z), including his bookcovers which are not often reproduced. A wider choice both in text and reproductions are to be found in *Montage: John Heartfield*, published by Elefanten Press in West Berlin as part of a project which included an exhibition and Helmut Herbst's film *John Heartfield, Photomonteur*, available with English subtitles through San Francisco Newsreel. I'd like to thank Tom Fecht at Elefanten for all his help. The Elefanten book also contains a very useful bibliography which should be used in conjunction with Friedrich Pfäfflin's bibliography of Heartfield's photomontages from 1930 through 1938, found in *Krieg im Frieden: Fotomontagen zur Zeit, 1930-1938*. Most recently, see *John Heartfield, Der Schnitt entlang der Zeit*, edited by Roland März and Gertrud Heartfield, from Verlag der Kunst, Dresden. For related material, see the special issue on A-I-Z of *Ästhetik und Kommunikation*, January 1973.

Thanks to Steve Stamos of Bucknell University and Lucy Lippard for their early letters of support; Ruth McCormick and Gwen Roginsky for assistance with translations; Mike Mosher for the lead on the audiotape battles in Poland; Dr. Illeana Leavens for the Poe reference; Nancy Linn for Kjelgaard; Gary Wilkie for Ehrendorf; Anne Gerber, James Mirel, and/or Service's Artists Projects in Seattle and the Goethe House in New York for their financial support; Elisa Manetti for support during the final stages of this project; C. L. Feringer, Brian Branagan and Ceric for assistance in manuscript preparation and to Robert C. Morgan for his helpful editorial suggestions. Finally, many thanks to Reese Williams of Tanam Press who asked me to undertake this project and then was patient beyond belief.

Tysk hatsang: Hvad raker os russer eller franskmand . . .

German song of hate: What matters to us the Russian or the Frenchman.

Deutscher Haßgesang: Was schert uns Russe und Franzos . . .

Chanson de haine allemande: Nous nous fichons des Russes et des Français.

From Ernst Friedrich, *Krieg dem Kriege* (1924)

WWI TO LATE WEIMAR

Radicalized Bohemia

> Those were the days of ersatz honey with an Iron Cross on the label,
> when we spread so-called war jam on our bread.
>
> —George Grosz

> We were then moving into a new world as into a new flat.
>
> —Viktor Shklovsky

In antebellum Berlin the garrets could be had for cheap. The Bohemians thus formed a stratum elevated over the middle classes housed below.

> Only solid, order-loving citizens lived in the four and five story houses. . . shopkeepers, doctors, government officials. But above them, under the roofs, we lived, Berlin's bohemians. . . . We felt ourselves nearer the cosmos, the eternal, unalterable beyond the powers-that-be.

Descending, they'd make their way to the Cafe des Westens— "The world outside called it Cafe Highfalutin' while the world inside called itself German Literature."[4]—and the Romanische Cafe, i.e., Cafe Megalomania. Here the Who's Who of Berlin literati spent their days and nights shaking the foundations of Western culture with a poem or capturing a world shaker with a quick, short stroked sketch. At the Cafe des Westens cultural migrants from Vienna "Karl Krauss and Adolf Loos are introducing their latest discovery to the Berliners—Oskar Kokoschka. When somebody fails to make out a vein on a head 'Koko' has drawn, he says: 'It's a beastly worm.'"[5]

As WWI approached it was embraced with an enthusiasm befitting the Expressionism rampant in the cafes. Those not terribly enthused could do little to avoid the physical sweep of nationalism. Less than two months into the fighting premier members of these circles began to fall. While assigned to a medical unit the poet Georg Trakl witnessed in the last poem before his own death "dying warriors, the wild complaint of their broken mouths."[6] A similar fate awaited numerous artists and intellectuals. They "were buried somewhere and rotting and with them also the work they might have created."[7]

For the respectable breed of German intelligentsia the war was to assure a perceived dominance of German culture and extend its cognitive Lebensraum past discrete national borders.

> As representatives of German Science and Art, we hereby protest to the civilized world, against the lies and calumnies with which our enemies are endeavoring to stain the honor of Germany in her hard struggle for existence—in a struggle which has been forced upon her. . . . Those who have allied themselves with Russians and Serbians and present such a shameful scene to the world as that of inciting Mongolians and Negroes against the white race have no right whatever to call themselves upholders of civilization. . . Have faith in us! Believe that we shall carry on this war to the end as a civilized nation, to whom the legacy of a Goethe, a Beethoven and a Kant is just as sacred as its own hearths and homes.[8]

". . . the ninety-three respected German artists and professors [who signed this statement] at the outbreak of the war voluntarily attested to '*their* Kaiser' that Germany's war was a just one and that all non-Germans were some kind of vermin on the face of the earth."[9] To Richard Huelsenbeck the "93" belonged to a larger "cultural association of psychopaths who. . . marched off with a volume of Goethe in their knapsacks to skewer Frenchmen and Russians on their bayonets."[10] Walter Benjamin saw among their type "the habitues of chthonic forces of terror who carry their volumes of Klages in their packs."[11] One soldier might have best captured the true significance of the intellectuals' statement when he wrote in his diary, "for five days my shoes have been slippery with human brains."[12]

While at the Flanders front Erwin Piscator carried the anti-militarist literary journal *Die Aktion* in his knapsack. Its international array of contributors formed a stratum elevated over governmental conflict, a de-classed internationalism which Wieland Herzfelde, John Heartfield's brother, recounted some years later

> The Russian Chagall, the Frenchman Appolinaire, they were close to us, they felt and searched as we did. The officers and the professors, the bankers and the trustees, even if they happened to speak German, what difference did that make to us? They had only sneers and disdain for our poems and paintings. How could they expect enthusiasm or "sacrifice of blood and toil" from us?. . . . No matter what the war was about, it was not about art or things of the spirit—we didn't call it fate—we called it madness, crime, murder!

This disposition had been influenced by the proletarian internationalism of Karl Liebknecht, the son of Marx's close associate Wilhelm Liebknecht and the sole Social Democrat in the Reichstag to vote against war credits. At a large Workers Day rally in Berlin on 1 May 1916 when he "appealed publicly for the struggle against the war, he gained the passionate veneration of rebellious, mostly young artists:"[13]

> Our enemies are not the English, French or Russian workers but the great German landed proprietors, the German capitalists, and their executive committee, the government.[14]

Piscator was working in a front-line theater group when he met Herzfelde, "a young man with full lips and most unmilitary bangs."[15] Herzfelde had originally volunteered for the medical corps as a compromise with carnage because "a medical orderly cannot be a murderer, or so I thought. So I played my part in the mass murders of Flanders 1914-15. . . . I saw them lying on beds of stinking straw, breathing their last in blood and filth. And my eyes began to open. I began to get more and more difficult, contradicted my superiors, felt I was an 'accessory to murder.' When he lashed out at his "own feelings of self-contempt, the result was peculiar: by the end of January 1915 I was sent home, a physically healthy returned soldier 'not worthy to wear the Emperor's uniform' anymore." Before being sent to the front once again in June

1916 he started the literary journal *Neue Jugend*, in part because the censors were watching *Die Aktion*, mainly to encourage opposition to the war.

Since it was necessary to obtain special permission to start a new journal during the war, Herzfelde acquired the imprimatur of a school boys magazine which had appeared previously only six times in 1914 before going defunct. To maintain this cover, so to speak, he began his first issue as issue #7, page 127, where the boys' magazine left off.

The contributors included many German Expressionists, the future ranks of Berlin Dada, the romantic socialist Gustav Landauer, and artists from outside Germany; Jouve, Seurat, Ensor, Chagall— in other words: "All European artists and intellectuals who are not senile, sober and submissive are invited to contribute and help."[16]

At the Romanische Cafe "the sacred muse of the German avant-garde", Else Lasker-Schüler, mourned the death of George Trakl and despaired the fact that her friend Helmut Herzfeld (Heartfield's given name) lacked the minimal acting abilities to feign mental incompetency, the tried and true method for avoiding the conscription notice he had just received. In response she schemed with friends to convince him that he was indeed a mental case. Upon his last visit to the cafe, as he sat at their table, they methodically failed to comprehend anything he said, responding in a sickly nurturing manner. The next time his brother Wieland saw him he was garbed in hospital stripes raking leaves. He was later discharged from the hospital, full wits about him, "suitable for labor utilization" and assigned to domestic duty as a mailman. "He lightened his duties in a meaningful but very risky manner: to make the people in Gruenwald wait in vain for the mail and, consequently, to enrage them at the conditions of the war, on a quiet street John stuffed whole bundles of mail and newspapers into the drain intended for rain water."[17]

The same year Wieland met George Grosz, who was posing as a "merchant from Holland" peddling an idea to make money through the sale of decoratively painted shrapnel. At the painter Ludwig Meidner's studio Wieland introduced him to Helmut, forming a trio lasting throughout their lives in spite of later political differences. After Helmut got a good look at Grosz's rapier-witted drawings his own artwork was suddenly superfluous. So he destroyed it. Grosz in return was impressed by Helmut, especially his anti-militarist aggravation via ditching the mail. Grosz mustered up his own method of aggravation by sending soldiers at the front individualized gift packages. Piscator was sent a stiffly starched dress shirt, gloves, tie, a request for exotic teas: all the requisite fineries while leaning up the side of a trench. Wieland recalls such a package at the end of 1916, "The parcel contained two starched shirt fronts, one white, the other flowered, a pair of cuffs, a dainty shoehorn, a set of bags of tea samples, which, according to hand-written labels, should arouse patience, sweet dreams, respect for authority, and fidelity to the throne. . . . Glued on a cardboard in wild dis-order were advertisements for trusses, fraternity song books, and enriched dogfood, labels for Schnapps and wine bottles, photos from illustrated magazines—arbitrarily cut out and absurdly joined together."[18]

The mail arrives (at least in this form of aggravation) disrupting the daily life at the front, an enforced attendance which, if left unchallenged, threatens to become routine punctuated by heroics and death. The trivia enclosed from the home front acts to trivialize the decimation at the front by displaying what exactly the fighting is meant to preserve. The fact that the raw encounters at the front resist trivialization results in a plague upon both the front and home front houses.

Only when compared to the war's exaggerated presence could a parcel's collection of irrelevancies achieve any critical depth. A similar dynamic can be observed in a passage from Egon Erwin Kisch's memoirs, *Sensation Fair*.

I had to lead a detail of men to the company quartered at our left. I asked a lance corporal, who had just turned aside in order to relieve himself, the direction to the company headquarters. With his free hand he gestured in the direction we had to take.

At almost that very instant the earth heaved. My mouth and my eyes were full of clumps of earth. When I was able to open my eyes again, it was to see the torso of the lance corporal lying on the earth with blood spurting like a fountain from his neck. A shell had gone through his head and sunk itself into the earth. It was a dud.

Back in my dugout, with my limbs still shaking, I noticed that my pants were bespattered with blood. I quickly reached for my paper in order to forget everything.

"It is easy to understand," I read, "why yesterday's auction, which disposed of the effects of the late Baron Wladimir Schlichtner, did not put up for public sale the famous snuffbox decorated with a risquè scene by the hand of Fragonard." —"The coming Sunday match between the 'Sport Chums' and the 'German Football Club,' who played it out to a tie in a heavily contested game last autumn, is keeping all the fans in suspense, all the more because. . ." . . .A soldier bleeding from the mouth, begged for water. Luckily there was still a little cold coffee in my canteen. He drank and stumbled on. I wiped his blood from the mouth of my bottle.

"Java sugar firm, 23.6 bid. Silver, 24.62 bid, 24.64 asked. Rotterdam (Fats and Oils) Turnover 6500. . .Court Brief: Judge Gericke of the Court of Domestic Relations Praises 24-Year-Old Martha Planer as "Model Daughter. . . ."

The odor of corpses had become unedurable. Heaven only knew when the pioneers would come to bury them.

"*Theatrical Section*: Fans of Pauline Ulrich, who are legion, will greet with joy the news that this star of the Dresden stage is to. . . . —Tomorrow evening that perfectly delightful operetta *The Clarinet-Girl*, will have its seventy-fifth consecutive performance, a record run for. . . — Our painful lack of a good contralto bids fair to be overcome with the arrival of Fräulein Helen Winterfield, formerly of Breslau. Those who have suffered. . ."

Sss-boom! A shell burst near our first-aid station. Sss-boom! Another much nearer to us. Sss-boom! A third cleaned up our latrine. We waited for the fourth.

"*Personals*: The blonde lady in the gray tailor-made suit, who surely noticed the gentleman who followed her, is urgently requested. . ." [...]"Suicide Pact in Double Love Tragedy" is the caption over a long sob-sister account of two school girls at the Weinberger Commercial School who tried to kill themselves because they were both in love with the same teacher. "Double Love Tragedy" indeed! If that was tragedy, then I ask you what word you have left to describe what we experience day after day at the front?[19]

Kisch was a very well known Communist journalist during Weimar, one who employed a variety of literary techniques, including montage of the type above. But montage is not merely technique limited to an immediate object or text; the disruptions, dislocations and conflations which montage entails operate socially as well. The disruption achieved in Kisch's battlefront representation by a systematic, if simple, technique was achieved also by Grosz's home front-to-front social intervention in the form of the parcels. Whereas the parcels and the "arbitrarily cut out and absurdly joined together" cardboards lacked the internal coherence and critical direction of a text like Kisch's, unlike such a text they were not directed over safe literary terrain but brazenly ventured into the center of the conflict.

In a vein which approached positive features of both, Grosz and Heartfield began to piece photos and words onto postcards to form anti-war messages sent to the front. Heartfield stated that the reason they took on a composite pictoral form was that similar messages written discursively would have been intercepted by the visually illiterate censors.

One reason these postcards could pass through the mail was that they resembled photomontaged postcards and carte vistas circulating during that time, usually glorifying the war or Kaiser, and reminding soldiers they were fighting for the wife, kids and country (incl. truss and dogfood) back home. All this gives perspective to Grosz's neutered (and oft quoted) statement— "When John Heartfield and I invented photomontage in my Southside studio at five o'clock in the morning. . ."[20] These primitive photomontages did not mythically spring forth from artistic inspiration and then settle down into an ascribable authorship for the edification of the future; they arose tactically in a context of dissent.

While Grosz and Heartfield were disrupting front/home front communications the war was making dramatic incursions into domestic dialogue. Cordial greetings were graced by a phrase from an Ernst Lissauer poem; "Gott strafe England," i.e. God punish England, followed by "He shall punish." Ostensibly, one could then get into discussing the weather secure under a chauvinist umbrella. In response, Helmut Herzfeld Anglicized his name to John Heartfield (not for love of England as an Englishman would later claim). He applied to have his new name legally registered. This was rejected by the empire. However, as Wieland noted, "A few years later the German people rejected the empire. The name Heartfield proved more durable.

The following year Heartfield again appealed to the state and again confronted a censor. Wieland was at the front leaving his

NEUE JUGEND

IM JUNI 1917

PR 2 P

PROSPEKT
zur Kleinen Gross Mappe.

prospekt zur Kleinen Gross Mappe.

Der Malik-Verlag Berlin-Südende

34, Steglitzer Strasse

CHRONIK

Friedrich Adler ist zum Tode verurteilt, Stockholm-Getöne gegen internationale Teuerung - das Leben weiterhin b Lebensmittel bleiben in Cornerstimmung. Nach Reuter verhungern in Ovamboland die Ovambos, keine Kaffern - European Dominions niemand! Verhungert doch - Steigerung!! Spinoza ist eingestampft für Bedarf diplomatischer Sendschreiben - L Pseudoliberia - Molière verriesselt in Sternheim (Zukunft vom 26. 5. 1917), Umfassungsmanöver gegen Wallner in Wien, Durst! - das A buch ist erschienen. Frühlingswende fiebert Sexualität, Heufieber. Liebeloh la l'au! Sich hinzu-schmeissen! Lichtmord!! — unsere sind so wund. Amokläufer . . . . Die Messer raus !!!

Man muß Kautschukmann sein!

Ja, Kautschukmann sein — eventuell den Kopf zwischen die Beine stecken oder durchs Faß springen — und spiralig in die Luft schnellen! sieh, ein Paragraph rempelt Dich an,
eine Affiche,
ein Flohzirkus —

(sämtliche Flöhe liegen an Schlingen desertieren ausgeschlossen — Springen von Flöhen auf Kommando, Paradenarsch der Flöhe . . . .)

EIN „MARSIAS" INTERESSENT

Immerhin wichtig ist, das Gleichgewichtzu behalten! Wo vordem die gotische Kirche, messelt sich heute das Warenhaus hoch — . — Die Fahrstühle sausen . . . Eisenbahnunglücks, Explosionskatastrophen — quer durchraus die Balkanzug Mitteleuropa, doch gibts auch Baumblüte und Edelmarmeladenrationierung — .

Wie gesagt, Kautschukmann sein beweglich in allen Knochen nicht blos im Dichter-Sessel dösen oder vor der Staffelei schön getönte Bildchen pinseln.

Den Bequemen gilts zu stören beim Verdauungsschläfchen ihm dem pazifistischen Popo zu kitzeln, rumort! explodiert! zerplatzt! oder hängt euch ans Fensterkreuz Laßt euren Kadaver in die Branntweingasse baumeln! Ja! Wieder elastisch werden, nach allen Seiten höchst federnd — sich verbiegen — anboxen! Kinn- oder Herzgrubenhieb!

Ladies and gentlemen!! jeder hat Zutritt!!

Nur nähertreten !! . . . nur nähertreten !! . . .
Schon beulen sie den Weihrauchkessel ein.
Nervös rutscht das weiche Gesäß hin und her!
Ja! Wenn nicht sämtliche Flöhe an Schlingen lägen!

Dieses Blatt ist der

PROSPEKT ZUR KLEINEN GROSZ-MAPPE

Die Sekte 1917

Die Sekte Neunzehn Siebzehn wächst aus dem Intellekt der umstehenden Zuhörer empor und zwingt ihre Mitglieder gegen den Block der Überzeugten. Die ohnmächtige Wut unserer Leser verpflichtet, einen bereits in Schwingung umgesetzten Glauben wieder zu fixieren, um mit den Gläubigen von neuem dagegen loszugehen. Die Leute wollen halt nichts alleine tun.

Sekten. Mehr Sekten. Noch mehr Sekten.

Das Wunder der Christian Science ist über unseren kürzlich veranstalteten Werbe Abend gerauscht und schüttet Glück aus über diejenigen, die uns lieben, um uns hinterrücks zu erdolchen.

Darum muss Einer seine Stimme erheben: Nicht mehr glauben, überhaupt nicht glauben. Sich selbst. (Sich und selbst) Beten.

Wenngleich jeder schuldig ist an der Unfähigkeit der andern, Feind zu sein, sondern schlotternder Neidhammel, soll keiner an dieser Schuld sich selbst beruhigt genug sein lassen. Nicht das Peinliche dieser Schuld schmatzend zu fressen, soll es ankommen, sondern Genuss auch noch auszukotzen — und wiederum zu fressen und wiederum!

Es ist in jeder Sekunde, die ein hundertmalverfluchtes Leben schenkt (unsägliche Wonne durch das galizische Petroleumgebiet zu durchfahren, die Gestänge der Bohrtürme verrusst!) so unendlich vieles zu tun.

Betet mit dem Schädel gegen die Wand!!

Wir — aha! — wir treten gegen die Menschen nicht auf. Wir treten geduldig noch mit den Menschen auf. Die Sekte Neunzehn Siebzehn schlägt gegeneinander, Sturmflut aus unseren Gebeten, die aus der Ohnmacht der Gläubigen emporgewachsen sind. Unsere Mitglieder verrecken, weil die Sekte sie nicht mehr locker lässt. Betet aus

98.8 Tempelh.
TELEPHON

REKLAMEBERATUNG

unseren Gebeten zu diesem Ende. Damit ihr endlich in die Schlinge kommt. Es ist ein so ungleiches Spiel mit diesen Sanften, Zappelnden. Der Magen der Neunzehn Siebzehn will das alles nicht mehr verdauen, immer wieder dasselbe, die Ohnmacht der Gläubigen, der Block der Ueberzeugten, das Einfangen, Verarbeiten, Auskotzen, Fressen,

das Ich triumphierend über Arenas, Michigan See, Sacha Sorau. Dort wurde der H Heinrich Steinhausen geborer in der Zeitung.

Halt dich, Junge.

Die Frist ist um. Her die Ladung. Sektierer, los! zappeln schon wieder?

Die Arbeit Arbeit Arbeit A Triumph der Christian Sc

Das Wunder der Sekte N Siebzehn.

1917.

SCHREIT!!

Kannst du radfahren

Zu den reinsten unverbildeten Erklärungen und unseres Lebens gehören jene Bilder auf den Rück Häuser, diese Erlasse des Kaufmanns (des wahren B Zeit) — von unerhörter Sachlichkeit vorgetragen, gegr geätzt wie auf alten Pyramiden, pressen sie das psy und formale Erleben des in knallenden Stadtfarb rollenden. Fabelhaft bunt und klar, wie nie ein T — von kosmischer Komik, brutal, materiell, bleiche waschen — dröhnend und mahnend gleich Ragtime ludie immer wieder sich im Gehirn bohrend —

Das gröhlt in einem fort!

Zwingt uns zum prallenden Marineblau, zu Grü Straßen Buchstaben), Varietégrün, Spezialitätengelb, grau, und füstelndes Rosa —

Mozialtönen tauchen auf . . . . .

Champagner-Flasche — der Korken knallt davo

Sekt Schloss Vaux

Ich, Dannemann-Zigarre schiel im Maul, Zeitung knerzen die Knattermotore — hart überholt mich B rote Autobus!

Ho! ho! schon wieder brüllen die Häuserwand Regie-Zigaretten, **Satrap**, Palast-Hotel Thomas, **bade zu Hause**, Steiners Pa bett . . . ho! . . . Sarg's Kaloo Passage-Café . . . . **AEG**

ja, vom Training kommend, am Punching Bal Joe hiebst Du nieder.

z. B., Du segeltest labelhaft in die Chaussee, eber Dir der Fußball an die klemmerlose Nase, Du im Aeroplan unter der Bergsonne — zwischen d knallte Deine Winchesterbüchse (Gott ließ ja Lu bravo)

Abends in den Asphaltbrüchen, in Geldsack-Hi Porter- Bierplakaten, oder an der Bar bei Kantorow quellen oder pikeln mit steilem Hemd aalglatt bei mendes Pils Cocktails Ersatz und Agoston, theater und Kinohäuser und d der beiden Herzfelder!

Sag mal! — **graults Dir** da in Kunstsalo Ölgemäldegalerien in den feinrussigen Soireen — .

Lieber Leser! Ein guter Fußballspieler enthä ganze Menge Wert — obwohl er nicht dichte Töne setzt!

Bleibt die Frage?

Kennst Du Schiller und Goethe — ? — ja!

Aber kannst Du radfahren?

Weitere Marsyas-Interessenten wollen sich noc

brother to direct the operations of *Neue Jugend*. Its increasing political profile had resulted in a ban. Heartfield reasoned in a letter to the Prussian censor General von Kessel:

> The *Neue Jugend* has been banned. In it a novel called *The Malik* by Else Lasker-Schüler was appearing in installments. We are under contract to publish the whole novel which is the story of a Turkish prince, in other words an *Ally*. We beg permission to open a publishing firm with the sole aim of publishing this novel. The firm would bear the name of the novel to be published—the Malik Verlag.[21]

The General might have been confusing a literary contract with a diplomatic pact. Whatever the reason, by turning wartime conceit against itself, permission was granted and, unknown to either party, what was to become the leading German publishing house of international leftist literature was founded.

During this time Heartfield was still "suitable for labor utilization," living in a barracks, while Herzfelde "read the proofs during a heavy bombardment of the Witchaete sector in Flanders."

> Not surprisingly, we could do nothing personally about distribution. This was handled for us superbly by the firm of Georg Stilke, Berlin. It had the monopoly for all railway bookshops and agencies serving the army. We delivered a complete sample edition to it for nothing, folded so that none of the contents could be seen. Sure enough, the paper reached Jerusalem, Warsaw, Northern Italy and Ostende. German organization. . . ![22]

The resourcefulness displayed by the acquisition of the existing imprimatur, sidestepping censorship, gaining transport in a monopoly market, let alone *Neue Jugend's* publication by its dispersed editors, was paralleled in Heartfield's design work. Franz Jung considered him "the life and soul of the operation," since "people bought it purely because of its layout. It was a sight for sore eyes: being in four colors one time, black paper with white lettering the next."[23] After the ban was lifted, it went to large newspaper, "American format," whereas previous numbers had been in a journal format common to avant-garde publications of the time.

The second "weekly" *Neue Jugend* appeared June 1917 disguised as a "Prospectus for the Little Grosz Portfolio." Heartfield's advertising for the portfolio appeared on the backside, a skull-and-

n nicht so gut wie vor wenigen Monaten

vorzuheben, eine Nummer allerersten Ranges. Fabelhafte Durcharbeitung von Grotesk-Wirkungen Ferner die Spaßmacher **Adolf und Coco.** Die Zuhörer werden in die überaus einfache Handlung der Komik unweigerlich eingefangen, die Ruhe Adolfs ist der größten Wirkung sicher. Die vornehme Selbstbeherrschung des Direktors Albert Schumann in seinem hervorragend gearbeiteten Dressurakt ist zu bekannt, als daß noch besondere Worte darüber zu verlieren wären. Gut sind auch die **4 Veras,** Drahtseilkünstlerinnen. Sie wirken in der Manege fast noch besser, als unlängst im Apollo-Theater. Das übrige ist Kriegsdurchschnitt. Dem großen Publikumg efallen **Turl Damhofers** Bayrische Alpen-Spiele. (Die Tauben auf der Szene schlagen gottseidank das Theater aus dem Feld). Die Pantomine **Halali,** Parforce-Schnitzeljagd, gehört nicht gerade zur besten Tradition des Unternehmens.

tionen der **gerade führenden** Verleger. An... Spitze marschiert die deutsche Handelsgesellschaf... undso, Abteilung Verlag, die neben dem Orkan g... eine ganze Romanserie verlegen will. Die Aufma... spottet jeder Beschreibung, jeder Marienkalende... besser. Paul Adler, im Zeichen höchster „Deutsch... — sagt er, hat das Wort!

Heinrich Michalski, Gründer von Beruf, ha... der Europäischen Staats- und Wirtschaftszeitung... gehabt — er ist trotz Gründung ausgebootet wo... Dort sitzen jetzt andere Herren am Tisch. Es ist z... grüßen, daß Heinrich bald was Neues gemanage... **Die Drei!** Sehr bescheiden. Michalski sollte... sagen: Die Tausend! Man lese aber dies Blatt, c... München mit irgendwelcher Politik und sonstwi... scheint. Man lese es um Heinrichs willen.

eben
schienen!

Soeben
erschienen!

oeben
schienen!

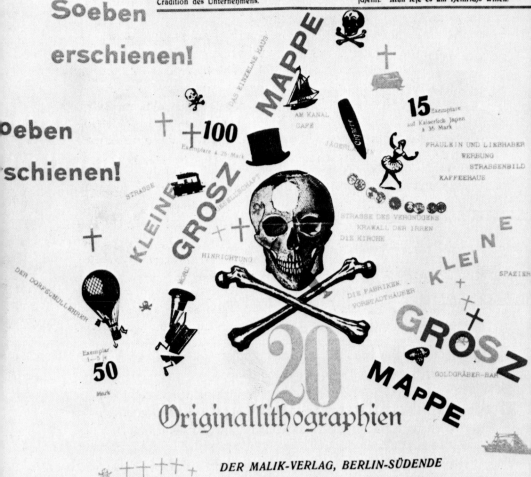

Prospectus for the Little Grosz Portfolio

crossbones trumpeting "Soeben erschienen!" —Just Published!—
20 Original Lithographs. The aleatoric rubber stamps, typing and
typography bear the mark not simply of cubistic simultaneity but of
the commercial compendium which brings everything to the simultaneity of exchange. Cubism, afterall, has been credited for
bringing commercial signage, thus the vulgarizations and negation
of social reality, into the spectacle of art. Heartfield reversed the
process. Instead of introducing, say a theater ticket into the frame
of a painting Heartfield took the practices of art outside the frame
to counter commercialism and its ideography upon its own terrain
in a newspaper of "American format."

A more direct influence was Grosz' own graphic work, especially in a work such as "Memory of New York," published in
Malik's *First Grosz Portfolio* in 1916. The frenetic overlays of an
urban setting he had never encountered except in reproductions
included the signage in English of: "Importers. . . Chicago Beach
Hotel. . . Oriental Danzing. . . Peppermint Gum: the best." Heartfield's dual background in commercial and fine art equipped him
with the skills and understandings to effect the same type of combination.

However, despite the displacement into a counter-
commercialism and any significance it might have had for art of
the time it was still an advertisement and lacked, outside of its
context and the lithos it promoted, a critical component commensurate with the war which still raged. Advertisings appearing
elsewhere did, unwittingly, relieve this shortcoming. *Die Aktion*
printed such adverts in a column called "Cuttings of the Time."
One reprinted from the Social Democratic newspaper *Vorwärts*
read: "War invalids with arm wounds, sound legs wanted immediately to crush Sauerkraut."[24]

In conjunction with the magazine, "*Neue Jugend* evenings" were
held. They served more as anti-war agitation than as propaganda
for the paper. At one evening a well-known actress read the last
lines of a poem entitled "Human Sacrafice"—

I was born the Kaiser's, went and soldiered
And a mother lost her son.
One?! Millions of sons died and mouldered
And the Kaiser's cruel sun shone on.[25]

Herzfeld describes the aftermath. "Tremendous excitement seized hold of the people. There were shouts of 'Down with the War! Down with the Kaiser!', women screamed and wept. People were carried out fainting." Pandemonium continued until police closed down the building.

The poem had been written by the Herzfelds' deceased father Franz Herzfeld (pseud. Held). In 1895 he had been convicted of blasphemy for a poem he had written. With his wife, Alice Stolzenberg, a textile worker and labor organizer, and their children he fled to Switzerland, settling later in the Austrian Alps. There the parents abandoned their children to a series of foster homes. "With this background," Hans Kleinschmidt recently wrote in a fit of cold war pyschotropics, "the cause of socialism becomes understandable."[26]

Accompanied by Grosz and Piscator, Heartfield and Herzfelde were among the first to join the German Communist Party, receiving their cards from Rosa Luxemburg at the founding congress on 31 December 1918. They woke up Communists in 1919. 1919, Year One of Dada as Raoul Hausmann put it. Only fifty other Berliners signed up as early, a select participation which must have given the impression of a fused avant-garde and vanguard with an ideational and operant history in reach, the future *in nuce*, if merely at this point to add real teeth to the Bohemian "epater le bourgeois".

Barely a year after the October Revolution in Russia the Keil sailors' refusal to embark on one last suicide mission sparked the so-called November Revolution in Germany. The exuberance that had once greeted the war now greeted its dissolution. It too was short-lived because defeat in the war did not bring substantive defeat to those who had fostered it. The Social Democratic Party (SPD), suddenly reformed after their entrenched support of the war effort, made a preemptive declaration of a republic literally hours before Karl Liebknecht of the Sparticists proclaimed a soviet republic. The SPD headquartered itself in the Reichstag toward the west while the Sparticists had taken over the Kaiser's Imperial Palace to the east, as it turned out, in proximity to their respective geopolitical alignments.

While facing west the SPD clung to the past, enlisting the imperial military, judiciary and civil servants, the industrialists and estate owners. The revolutionaries, with a taste of the November Revolution in their mouths, set out to rid the Imperial residue and achieve actual revolution. In some of their first actions they took over the newspaper offices of Ullstein, Mosse, Scherl and, on Christmas 1918, the Social Democratic *Vorwärts*. There they issued "The Red Vorwärts", printing it on red paper. Four days later the Social Democrat Gustav Noske joined the provisional government replacing the Independent Socialists who had been purged. On 11 January he led an army regiment in the shelling of the occupied *Vorwärts* building. Those surrendering were shot with hands and white flags over their heads. Noske was aided in this mission and many missions to follow by the Freikorps, the violent and nationalistic "vanguard of Naziism" sanctioned by the SPD. On 15 January Freikorps officers and a few of their friends assassinated Rosa Luxemburg and Karl Liebknecht.

A couple days after the assassination Wieland met with Count Harry Kessler, a diplomat and arts patron, to discuss the publication "of a new periodical of a literary, artistic and political character, brought out at irregular intervals, cheap (not more than fifty pfennings per number), newspaper-style make-up but in accordance with [Wieland's] own typographical ideas, and directed in the first instance toward street sales." The intent according to Wieldand was "to sling mud at everything that Germans have so far held dear."[27] The result was *Jedermann sien eigner Fussball* (Everyman his own Football), Malik Verlag's first post-war publication. It appeared only once on 15 February 1919 in newspaper format at a price of forty pfennings and distributed in a very unique manner on 17 February through the tense streets of Berlin. Walter Mehring recounts the distribution:

> We hired a char-a-banc [cart] of the sort used to Whitsuntide outings and also a little band complete with frock coats and top hats who used to play at ex-servicemen's funerals. We, the editorial staff, paced behind six-strong bearing bundles of *Jedermann sein eigner Fussball* instead of wreaths. In the sophisticated west end of the city we earned more taunts than pennies, but our sales mounted sharply as we entered the lower-middle class and working class districts of north and east Berlin. Along the street of dingy tenements riddled by

the machine gunfire of the Spartakus fighting and sliced open by the howitzers of the Noske regime the band was greeted with cheers and applause as it played its two star pieces which were the sentimental military airs. . . our Dadaist procession was greeted with delight as spontaneous as the *on y danse* of the Paris mob in front of the Bastille. And "everyman his own football" entered the Berlin language as an expression of contempt for authority and humbug.[28]

This procession resembled the numerous funeral processions which criss-crossed Berlin beginning in December 1918. It followed the route "to the dreary east side" as had Liebknecht's funeral one month earlier (Luxemborg's body was not recovered from a river until 31 May).

Heartfield designed *Jederman* and created two photomontages on the cover. The titular photomontage shows Wieland in formal attire spliced into a soccerball, graciously tilting his hat while saying "everyman his own football"— something of a sarcastic version of "a chicken in every pot." The main photomontage reads: "Open Competition! Who's the prettiest?? —German Manly Beauty #1." The open fan, very much from the 19th Century, shows members of the ruling Ebert-Scheidemann group along with Karl Kautsky, the patriarch of social democracy, surrounding General Ludendorff, the diehard animator of the Supreme Military Command during the war and future participant in the Kapp Putsch, and other military leaders. Apart from the radiant beauty emanating from the Imperial military to the ruling socialists, the Ebert-Scheidemann group were known among the Berlin Dadaists for their physiognomy of power, "gifted beer bellies" in Huelsenbeck's words. A typical jowl-ladden face was a "sleepy ass with beard trimming" according to Hausmann in *Der Dada 1*. The result of the contest to answer the question "who's prettiest?" was published in the heir of *Jedermann*, *Die Pleite* (Bankruptcy), the satirist Kurt Tucholsky won first prize.

This cover was Heartfield's first coherent employment of photomontage. As Wieland stated, "In it he began for the first time to use photography consciously in the service of political agitation." It was a number of years until Heartfield produced other photomontages of this moderate level of sophistication, not for another five years, and it was nearly ten until this level would be sustained and superceded.

Preis 40 Pf.

"Jedermann sein eigner Fussball"

Illustrierte Halbmonatsschrift

1 Jahrgang · Der Malik-Verlag, Berlin-Leipzig · Nr. 1, 15. Februar

Sämtliche Zuschriften betr. Red. u. Verl. an: Wieland Herzfelde, Berlin-Halensee, Kurfürstendamm 76. Sprechst.: Sonntags 12—2

Preisausschreiben!
Wer ist der Schönste??

Deutsche Mannesschönheit I

Die Sozialisierung der Parteifonds

Eine Forderung zum Schutze vor allgemein üblichem Wahlbetrug

Die Ausführungen sollen den Unfug unserer Nationalversammlung
im Gesichtspunkt der Demokraten aus illustrieren, jener Leute,
ein Volk dürfe keine Regierung besitzen, deren Niveau dem
der Dumnheiten überragen ist.

Man mag Demokrat sein, deutsch-sozialistischer Unterton oder Kommu-
nist, man mag mit Schiller sagen: Verstand ist stets bei wenigen nur
wesen oder behaupten auf jede Stimme komme es (sogar mit Recht)

Included in *Jedermann* was a cartoon by Grosz showing the pope holding puppets of the Chief Minister and the Chief Press Officer instructing them on the evils of Bolshevism. Grosz and Heartfield later made puppets for a Mehring play presented at the cabaret Schall und Rauch (Smoke and Noise) in the basement of Max Reinhardt's Deutsches Theater, where Heartfield was on the design staff. One of the puppets, Woodrow Apollon, a caricature of Woodrow Wilson, criticized Wilson's acquiesence to the Allies' harsh Versailles Treaty terms. During the war Herzfelde, Grosz and Heartfield had worked on a puppet film meant to satirize the United States' involvement but the film was scrapped when the original intent of the official film was reversed to criticize the Germans. In this vein, Heartfield's later montages can be seen as a puppetry using mass media reproductions instead of papier-mache.

Most of the 7,600 issues of *Jedermann* got sold on the procession but enough remained to be confiscated upon the arrest of its publisher on 7 March. Herzfelde was held without charge for two weeks during the height of renewed street fighting which resulted from a Communist call for a general strike and Noske's response to the strike. The 15,000 involved in the strike were met by 40,000 Freikorps; in the end 1,200 workers were dead.

Harry Kessler was told "that Wieland Herzfelde has been arrested for publishing in *Jedermann* the condemnation of the White Terror by the Bavarian Soldier's Councils." The condemnation of the White Terror by the Bavarian Soldier's Councils." The condemnation referred to was printed on the last page. It warned the revolutionaries of the Bavarian Soviet, "The revolution is in peril. Close ranks around your flag and for the fight against the White Terror of Berlin." A month-and-a-half later Noske's troops assaulted Munich, apprehending, Eugene Levinè, the Soviet's leader and friend of Heartfield and Herzfelde. In their proclamations the government asserted that they came "not as enemies of the working class, not as White Guards, but as protectors of public safety and order. . . . radical champions of the socialist movement."[29] On 5 June Levinè was executed.

Herzfelde described his experience for Kessler. "His descriptions of them are so dreadful that I felt sick with nausea and indignation. They exceed Dostoevsky's *House of the Dead*. The ill-treatment of prisoners, from being spat in the face to standing against the wall and being beaten to death, was so general and their torture in the presence of officers such a matter of course that Wieland's belief in trained lynching, with set instruction hours, almost seems to make sense. He says that the prisoners' bitternesss is so great that to plead for the life of a single bourgeois is downright dangerous. . . in the prevailing situation, and after what he has seen he feels it impossible to strike a lighthearted note in his periodical. Only a struggle waged with the most extreme means matters any longer." Grosz told Kessler that he had witnessed a soldier without papers shot "out of hand" in front of the Hotel Eden where Wieland was taken immediately upon arrest. A couple of days after Wieland was released Kessler chronicled a visit from Heartfield in his day-book: "A visit from Helmut Herzfeld. In connection with his periodical, he expressed his utter repugnance to the publication of poems by Däubler or Becher or indeed anything that is just art. He and his friends, he explained, are becoming more and more hostile to art."

Anti-Expressionism

The important man is not the artist, but the businessman who, in the marketplace and on the battlefield, holds the reins in his hands.
—John Heartfield[30]

On page 15 of der dada 3 there appeared a disarray of squiggles and dots entitled "Woman in Blue, XVII", headlined "Quintessential Expressionism" and "created" by Heartfield. For the Berlin Dadas there was nothing quintessential to be found in Expressionism because it was deeply inflicted by, among other ailments, the liberalness of Social Democracy. Both Expressionists and Social Democrats shared a general trajectory over the span of the war, initially embracing it despite antecedent positions which could have just as easily substantiated rejection, becoming disenchanted with the rising political and corporeal costs, meeting at the end of the war with a pacifism whose thoughtfulness sunk as deep as the monarchy. Class distinctions were buried in the soul of the Expressionist New Man or pragmatized into oblivion by Social Democratic reformism. After the war both ends of the Expressionist

35

ranks dissolved; many became Communists and other revolutionaries; others solidified into the SPD-sanctioned "Official Expressionism"—so many Kerenskis in smocks.

At the Cafe Grössenwahn Leonhard Frank punched out a person who was celebrating the sinking of the Lusitania. On the flipside of the war he was propagandizing for the New Man from exile in Switzerland. *Man is Good*, his book authored in exile and appearing in Germany early in 1919, became the solipsistic anthem for the Activist wing of Expressionism. The Activists' office immediately after the war was right near the New Fatherland League in the Reichstag, headquarters for the SPD and the new republic.

Amid street fighting during the Kapp Putsch a bullet entered a gallery and pierced a Rubens painting "Bathsheba." Oskar Kokoschka denounced the incident in a statement imploring the combatants "not to wage your warlike exercises in front of the art gallery at the courthouse but, perhaps, to hold them at the rifle range out in the field where human culture will not be endangered." (This is just the opposite of what Bakunin proposed for the 1849 Dresden insurrection. Paintings were to be taken from their sacrosanct locations and placed on the barricades just in case their presence would deter the advancing troups' bullets.)

Grosz and Heartfield included Kokoschka's statement in their rejoinder "The Bastard of Art" which appeared in Malik Verlag's *Der Gegner*. It addressed "the workers".

> After the Kapp Putsch, when you took up arms, much to the displeasure of the anti-militarists and pacificists who would have preferred to see you dressed in long white robes with a candle in one hand and Prof. Frank's book *Man is Good* in the other, organized against the repression of the swastika followers, preferring to rout the White Saviors by spiritual means. . .

Kokoschka was Official Expressionism incarnate, agonized innards framed with a professorship, the *enfant terrible* become bankable, an investment oasis amid the immiseration of early-Weimar's outrageous inflation.

> ". . . his picture *The Actress Margarete Kupfer with her Pet Dog* which can be painted from left or right without expressing anything bad for the bourgeois, which, when a so-called revolutionary expenditure of cobalt blue perchance runs out, can be continued with

Prussian blue and still function as a classic and in the art-conscious home of Mrs. Big Mill Owner. . ."

It didn't much matter what claims were made for Expressionism, the paintings still gravitated toward "luxurious panelling of lofty walls" or in front of wall safes, far from the "worker's louse-infested bed." (By 1937 photographs of Heartfield and Kokoschka were placed side by side in *Volks Illustrierte* with announcements that they were to be nominated as honorary members into the Czechoslovakian artists union "because of their merit to true German art.")

"The Bastard of Art" came toward the end of Berlin Dada and represented an explicitly political edge of the movement. Other Berlin Dada statements contra-Expressionism were generally not set against the rock bottom existence of the working class. Richard Huelsenbeck wrote in the first German Dada manifesto that the "best and most extraordinary artists will be those who *every hour snatch the tatters of their bodies out of the frenzied cataract of life*, who, with bleeding hands and hearts, hold fast to the intelligence of their time. . ." instead of, in "The Bastard of Art", the worker,

> . . .his comrades, his family, all his fellow strugglers, which, thanks to the bourgeois bloodsuckers and swollen boss toads he continually sees foundering, and feels guilty for *every minute which does not bring with it the liberation of the world from the slimy fangs of the capitalist system.*

Huelsenbeck covered many bases in his manifesto with the question, "Has expressionism fulfilled our expectations of such an art, which should be the expression of our most vital concerns? No! No! No!" Why not?

1. Because the Expressionists were "already looking forward to honorable mention in the histories of literature and art . . ."

Denying aspirations toward the future histories of art and literature was in immediate reaction to the superfluousness of well-groomed canons and of those individuals still walking Berlin streets who were being groomed as canon fodder. By denigrating these lesser histories they could also signal the magnitude of historical transformation they had in mind. The Berlin Dadaists, after-all, as radical intelligentsia in a period of giddy possibility, harbored broader backgrounds and involvements than just art and literature. If they were to enter history it would be with this extended pallette. Although this sentiment needed little time to betray itself for its tactical features, a degree of sincerity was evidenced by a lack of material evidence.

The Berlin Dadaists produced relatively few objects and left scant and conflicting records, except for Grosz. Heartfield was one of the central members of Berlin Dada, yet he left little tangible (marketable thus historicizable) record from those days. Heartfield once told Kessler that "he and his friends do not want either to document their actions or to create any kind of durable record and thus to impede posterity." What he left were collaborative ventures in publication, especially *dada 3*, or in collaborative artworks with Grosz—their collages, "Corrected Picasso" and "Corrected Rousseau." The cover of *dada 3* was signed John Heartfield mont.", and the title page on the April 1920 issue stated that the editors or "Directeurs" are an assembly of "groszfield, hearthaus, georgemann" after Grosz, Hausmann and Heartfield. A picture originally taken on the Universum Filmgesellschaft grounds showing him hugging a donkey's head, bearing the caption "Monteurdada JOHN HEARTFIELD instructs the Dada ass," was the first time Heartfield went public with his name "Monteurdada." *dada 3* was issued by Malik Verlag and Wieland, spliced in the selfsame soccerball that appeared on the cover of *Jedermann*, became an advertising, his words filling a flacid cartoon balloon, "Buy Malik-Verlag books and don't forget: Dada Conquers!!!"

2. Because an art "transformed into an opulent idyll and the expectation of a good pension has nothing in common with the effort of active men." Although the Expressionists harbor sentiment which should carry them to action, their "hatred of the press, hatred of advertising, hatred of sensations, are typical of people who prefer their armchair to the noise of the street. . . On the pretext of carrying on propaganda for the soul, they have, in their struggle with naturalism, found their way back to the abstract, pathetic gestures which presuppose a comfortable life free from content or strife."

The Berlin Dadas did not prefer the noise of the street; they chose rather to provoke and generate the noise. The funereal distribution of *Jedermann* is but one example. Johannes Baader showered the inauguration of the National Assembly with a flyer "The Green Corpse on the White Horse Dada" proclaiming himself the President of Germany by process of being President of the Globe. (In the spring of 1924 the KPD indulged in similar antiparliamentary actions when, attending the Reichstag outfitted in black shirts and red ties, they would toot toy trumpets when comments from the floor or podium displeased them.[31]) Hausmann and Baader at one time planned to found a Dada Republic at the Berlin suburb Nikolassee. They were to inform the mayor that on 1 April he was to evacuate his position, all large land owners were to be declared "futile bourgeois" and if anyone caused a stink there were 2,000 soldiers waiting on the outskirts of town. Their plan was abandoned; just as well, the mayor heard of the plan and on 1 April had 2,000 soldiers of his own to repel any assault. In 1923 one-time Dadaist Franz Jung hijacked a German freighter in the Baltic commandeering it to Petrograd as a present to Soviet Russia. (Perhaps the only precedent by a cultural figure was D'Annunzio's occupation of Fiume in 1919. The Berlin Dadaists apparently sent a telegram of congratulations.)

The Berlin Dada performances, unlike the single cabaret locale of Zurich Dada performances and like the traveling shows of the Russian Futurists, extended outside Berlin circuits to Dresden, Teplitz-Schonau and Prague. Grosz remembered one where "Walter Mehring would pound away at this typewriter, reading aloud the poem he was composing, and Heartfield or Hausmann or I would come from backstage and shout: 'Stop, you aren't going to hand out real art to those dumbbells, are you?'" On 24 May 1919, a "race between a sewing machine and a typewriter" was staged with Mehring again at the typewriter and Grosz at the sewing machine. Herzfeld remembers the event as a 1917 *Neue Jugend* evening where the sewing machine "sewed an endless band of mourning crepe symbolizing the vain fight to create war enthusiasm."[32] If politics weren't integral to the account given by Grosz they were at least contingent since the originally scheduled time for the performance was postponed in observance of a day of mourning for the judicial leniency shown the assassins of Liebknecht and Luxemburg.

3. Because the Expressionists' "propagandizing for the soul" resounded only as far as the rafters of the skull; their "struggle with naturalism" sent them retreating into a complete "renunciation of objectivity."

> "Dada is God and John Heartfield his prophet."
> —Poster at 1920 First International Dada Fair

In a conversation with the art historian Francis Klingender while exiled in England, Heartfield stated that "Dada was a revolt against the 'higher impulses. . . Dada came out of the experience of the 'powerlessness of the spiritual'—'the shooting goes on.'"

> In 1917 Dada was nihilistic. The spiritual needed to be destroyed, but only in order to forge ahead to reality. We must be concrete, name names; therefore, trouser buttons, newspaper clippings, parts of real objects.

Concrete objects signaled the Berlin Dada call for an objectivity (Gegenständlichkeit) bearing the aggressive markings of the Expressionism it countered. It influenced various strains of the "New Objectivity" and the politicized realism which opposed the former's mollified fetish for surface objectivity.

Expressionism and Berlin Dada were exhausted by the early 20s. Neue Sachlichkeit did not gain momentum until 1925 in the Stresemann period when Weimar experienced political and economic conditions stabilized by enormous loans. The acceptance of even Official Expressionsim was awkward and concessionary; Neue Sachlichkeit was a perfect fit. Its affirmation of surface discouraged scrutiny of the artificially buttressed status quo. It became the social realism for the liberal bourgeoisie.

What was once sufficient for Dada—invoking real objects— offered no contestation a little over five years later. As Heartfield told Klingender, "Neue Sachlichkeit: under the pretext of going back to real objects, social reality was sidetracked." In the interim, many of those involved with the obstinate objectivity of Dada were becoming seasoned in locating the relations underneath the surface of real objects, of names, of newspaper clippings. There they found turf populated by people, events and history.

Malik, Piscator, Münzenberg: Publishing, Theater, Print

The cultural policy of the German Communist Party was leftover from Franz Mehring and the earlier years of the SPD. Its main tenets were that a proletarian art would have to wait until the proletariat was raised out of immiseration. In the meantime the party was to tender the classical bourgeois heritage while fending off the cultural death throws of a fetid capitalism. Somewhat predictably then, the official organ of the KPD, *Die Rote Fahne* (The Red Flag—*DRF*), did not react favorably to the First International Dada Fair nor to those involved who were KPD members. After the early assassinations and expulsions in the party, the burdens of adventurous pursuits on inexperienced leadership left little time for pondering the way out of cultural retardation. The result was for the most part tolerance by neglect.

This proved to be fortunate since it required Communist artists to construct and participate within organizations and institutions "semi-autonomous" from the party. (Any talk of cultural autonomy from political parties must, of course, be compared to the submerged, fatuous autonomies of the present-day market which can keep a tighter tether under an appearance of greater freedom.) Once party policy turned toward more active involvement in cultural matters, beginning officially with the 1925 Tenth Party Congress and in full swing by the late 20s, it was contending with individuals and institutions with their own ideas and developments of a materialist aesthetic and proletarian artistic practice. Thus there was never a tenured practice of direct party intervention (the litterateurs would spawn their own hatchet men).

Heartfield developed and matured within such "semi-autonomous" surrounding institutions, even as he moved toward the center of KPD legitimacy and activity in the late 20s. The three of the most important were represented in the personages of Wieland Herzfelde, Erwin Piscator and Willi Münzenberg.

The first, Malik Verlag, Heartfield "founded" on 1 March 1917 during his deception of the war time censor. Malik was actually a continuation of Wieland's efforts beginning with *Neue Jugend*. The firm remained under his general direction from its very modest beginnings to its stature as the major Weimar publisher of international leftist writing and literature, until it was forced into exile—i.e., from ". . . the persecutions during the Spartakus battles, the prosecuting councils of the republic and Dr. Goebbels himself, who had approximately 400,000 Malik volumes confiscated. . ."[33] From exile in Prague and New York it came to rest in its final years in the German Democratic Republic.

During Weimar, Malik's activities were concentrated in three main areas: periodicals, art portfolios and books. Besides *Neue Jugend*, *Jederman sein eigner Fussball*, and *dada 3* Malik also published the periodicals *Die Pleite* (Bankruptcy) and, incorporating *Die Pleite*, *Der Gegner* (The Adversary). The detraction from Berlin Dada due to these publishing efforts prompted Hans Richter in his *Dada: Art and Anti-Art* to write that the "Herzfeldes, Grosz and [Franz] Jung were embarking on a conventional [!] career at the Malik-Verlag."

The first issue of *Die Pleite* carried the announcement for the First Congress of the Third International, a call by the Russian Minister of Culture Lunacharsky for coordination of efforts between German and Russian artists and, as in the issues to follow, attacks on the Social Democrats. *Der Gegner* came about in conjunction with Julian Gumperz who helped capitalize Malik in 1921, when choices between food and stamps were favoring the latter. When Gumperz left in 1924 Wieland noted the related departure of his own hair. It was not until the latter-half of the 20s that Malik was securely above water.

The publishing of Grosz's portfolios were responsible for much of the press noteriety. There were six portfolios published, some in special editions to fund other ventures; three of the six resulted in legal actions and decisions against Herzfelde and Grosz. There were also censorships of a number of Heartfield bookcovers which brought Malik further publicity.

Malik books covered a full range of genres and topics with a strong emphasis on translation (e.g., numerous Russian authors and a number of titles by Upton Sinclair) and reportage in journalistic and novel forms. During Weimar alone over 300 titles were published including works by Hausmann, Huelsenbeck, Jung, Johannes Becher, Dos Passos, Mayakovsky, Gorki, Trotsky, Kollontai (*The Ways of Love*), Isaac Babel, Ilya Ehrenberg, Tretyakov, Tolstoy, Wittfogel, Lukacs (*History and Class Consciousness*, *Lenin*), were published during the Weimar Republic alone.

Malik also operated a bookstore, the Malik Buchhandlung, an important meeting place for Weimar communist and leftist intellectuals and the object of several vandalisms. What is understood by some to be Heartfield's first political photomontage "Ten Years Later: Father and Sons" (August 1924) was designed for Malik Buchhandlung's window. "The montage was displayed in the shop window. . . surrounded by military proclamations, ration cards, illegal leaflets and other documents of WWI." (In a similar display in the windows of the publishing offices of Ernst Friedrich's *Freie Jugend*, approximately seventy photographs from Friedrich's book *Krieg dem Kriege* (War Against War), showing unsanitized scenes from the war, were removed by Berlin police on 30 September 1924.)

In 1933 Malik moved to Prague and continued publishing under London registry until 1939, the last title being Brecht's *Svendborg Poems*. Brecht's *Fear and Misery of the Third Reich* was the first title of Herzfelde's Aurora (i.e., red dawn) Verlag in New York where he also opened the Seven Seas Bookshop. He had hoped to produce books to be sent to German prisoners of war as well as publish *Faschistenspiegel* (Mirror of Fascism) by his brother but got around to neither project before leaving for the GDR in 1949, continuing there with Aurora Bucherei for a year until the time when he was once again joined by John.

Heartfield was Malik's art director and, along with Grosz, the in-house artist—although a couple other artists were involved, including Rudolf Schlichter, who worked with Heartfield at *Der Knüppel* and at *Die Rote Fahne* and is now remembered for the hanging pig-in-uniform at the First International Dada Fair and his later verist portraits. Working at Malik meant a continuing association with Wieland. They were jointly responsible for almost all the design work. It was a working relationship that extended over into Heartfield's photomontage work. As a writer, Wieland often supplied the text for Heartfield's photomontages in A-I-Z, many photomontages being little more than backdrop to a text or poem. There are indications that Wieland was in on formulating some of his brother's better known images as well.

Heartfield designed books and bookcovers for a large number of Malik titles. He started calling his early bookcovers "photomontages" although few of them contained composite photographs;

the ones that did were very simple and did not display the multi-form orchestrations familiar in his later on work (this sophistication would happen concurrent with his poster and photomontage work starting around 1928). He stated that the simple continguity of his often times highly ingenious graphic titles and the photographs satisfactorily constituted photomontage. This early bookcover work at Malik was of great significance in the development of his own work in that it required that a commercialist governor be applied to the wilder graphic and affective aspects which had been freely exercised during dada. The books, afterall, were not very big so the photographic images had to be centralized and simplified to attract attention on shelves and in the window displays. Malik also offered him the opportunity to work with photographs during the period of inflation.

At the end of inflation, Heartfield's work with Piscator would introject upon the site vacated by the restrained dadaist effluence a plethora of options, sources, formal organizational modes and aesthetic strategies.

Heartfield's design broke dramatically with the accepted notions of a bookcover's secondary or ancillary role. This was best demonstrated by Heartfield's willingness, at times, to change the title of the book to better suit either the book's content and/or the image he had in mind for the cover. Upton Sinclair's *Mountain City* became *How to Make Dollars*, Ehrenberg's *Ten Horse Power* became *The Life of Cars* and his *United Front* became *Most Sacred Possessions*.

Although up until his exile to England in 1938 the overwhelming percentage of Heartfield's book projects were with Malik, he did do work for Verlag für Literatur und Politik, Münzenberg's Neuer Deutscher Verlag and his Paris exile Edition du Carrefour among others. Titles included John Reed's *Ten Days that Shook the World*, Larissa Reissner's *October*, Michael Gold's *Jews Without Money*, Gladkov's *Cement*, books by Clara Zetkin, Anna Seghers, etc. While in England he worked on a very large number of books which almost entirely underutilized his artistic skills and alienated him from any political relevance, e.g. *Flowering Shrubs for Small Gardens*.

All told, his innovations changed the face of books and not just graphically. Walter Benjamin thought that "much of [Dada's] revolutionary content has gone into photomontage. You need only think of the work of John Heartfield, whose technique made the bookcover into a political instrument."[34] Kurt Tucholsky wrote in 1932 under one of his pseudonyms, "If I weren't Peter Panter, I'd like to be a bookcover in the Malik Verlag. This Johnny Heartfield really is a little wonder of the world." To date, however, his graphic innovations and achievements have been largely ignored by leftist graphic artists as well as the great appropriating vacuum of capitalist commercial arts.

Returning from the war, Piscator's first theater Das Tribunal staged Expressionist productions in Königsberg. He then moved to the outskirts of Dada amid the radical intensity of Berlin. In the fall of 1920, just weeks after the First International Dada Fair, he began the Proletarisches Theater, initiating agit-prop in Germany. The theater performed at working class venues, with amateur actors and with very few props or costumes. Der Gegner published the program for its first production which was held in Kliem's Dining Hall on the third anniversary of the Russian October Revolution. It featured a triple bill. One play was Russia's Day by an Hungarian refugee named Lajos Barta—a very coarse propagandistic play starring World Capital and his understudies Diplomat, Officer and Preacher. The workers eventually clear the stage of the aforementioned and destroy the national boundaries preventing all workers, including those in the audience, from joining in a rousing rendition of the Internationale. Heartfield designed the map of Europe and Russia, with the aforementioned national boundaries, as the backdrop of the play. He also designed the backdrop of another play on the bill, Karl Wittfogel's The Cripple, a play positing causes for the army of crippled veterans begging the streets of Germany.

Piscator affectionately (divorced for the while from the gist of the play) attributes the invention of Epic Theater to Heartfield's-late delivery of the backdrop for The Cripple.

"Stop, Erwin, stop! I'm here!" All hands turned in astonishment toward the little man with the red face who had just burst in. We could not simply go on, so I stood up, abandoned my role as the cripple for the moment and called down to him: "Where have you been all this time? We waited almost half an hour for you and then

46

we had to start without your backdrop." Heartfield, "You didn't send the car! It's your fault! I ran through the streets, the streetcars wouldn't take me because the cloth was too big. When I finally managed to board one I had to stand on the platform at the back and I almost fell off!" I interrupted him: "Calm down, Johnny, we have to get on with the show." Heartfield: "No, the cloth must be put up first!" And since he refused to calm down I turned to the audience and asked them what was to be done, should we continue or should we hang up the backdrop? There was an overwhelming majority for the backdrop. So we dropped the curtain, hung up the backdrop and to everybody's satisfaction started the play anew.[35]

Heartfield designed a number of sets for Piscator and got a taste of other skills since "the separate tasks of writer, director, musical director, designer and actor constantly overlapped." For *Trotz Alledem!* (*In Spite of Everything*, 1925) Heartfield's original plan called for a 65-foot battleship representing British imperialism to accompany a mammoth outdoor spectacle, the type of which had been developed in Russia—but the play moved indoors. Heartfield constructed "a terraced structure of irregular shape with a raked platform on one side and steps and levels on the other", placed it on a revolving stage and painted the entire apparatus uniformly brown. There was no scenery instead film and still photos were projected on the construction.

> . . . we used authentic shots of the war, of the demobilization, of a parade of all the crowned heads of Europe, and the like [obtained from a contact in the government archives]. These shots brutally demonstrated the horror of war: flame thrower attacks, piles of mutilated bodies, burning cities; war films had not yet come into "fashion", so these pictures were bound to have a more striking impact on the masses of the proletariat than a hundred lectures.

Piscator co-scripted the play with KPD emissary and dramaturg Felix Gasbara, a journalist and co-editor with Heartfield of the KPD satirical journal *The Cudgel*. The title *Trotz Alledem!* referred to Liebknechts phrase shortly before his assasination that "In Spite of Everything," i.e., the severe defeats of the Communists in 1919, the revolution continued. This was something to be pointed out since the 10th Party Congress had just ascertained that there existed "an acute revolutionary situation."

The sequence of scenes covered the period from the start of the war, when Liebknecht was the only Social Democrat voting against war loans, through the assassinations of Liebknecht and Luxemborg under the sanction of Social Democrats ". . . [the live scenes and film clips] interacted and built up each other's power and at intervals the action attained a *furioso* that I have seldom experienced in theater. For example, when the Social Democrats vote on War Loans (live) was followed by film showing the first dead, it not only produced a shattering human effect, it became art, in fact. What emerged was that the most effective political propaganda lay along the same lines as the highest artistic form."

Because of the collectivity involved in the production of this and other plays, just how much Piscator influenced Heartfield or vice versa is difficult to ascertain. The similarities this work has with Heartfield's mature work point to the fact that the work with Piscator was pivotal if only to provide Heartfield with an occasion.

Piscator's plays of the mid-20s, beginning with *Flags* (1924) and hitting full stride with *Trotz Alledem!*, heralded general artistic trends which came to fruition in the late 20s and early 30s. These trends contended at first with a burgeoning Neue Sachlichkeit and became more active as the socio-economic underpinnings of the republic gave way to the approaching depression. During this latter phase Heartfield began to consistently produce the photomontages for which he is known. Leo Lania described the beginning of these cultural trends in an article on Piscator's *Flags*, entitled "Art Desecrated": "The de-romanticization of art has prepared the way for the romanticization of everyday life, and the way leads from "pure art" to journalism, to reporting, from poetry to truth, from the invention of sentimental fables or dabbling in the secrets of psychology to insistent, true-to-life descriptions of the exciting mysteries of prisons, factories, offices, machines, added values and the class struggle."[36]

Specific to Heartfield in Leo Lania's description was the movement leading away "from 'pure art' to journalism, to reportage." This step outside conventionally proscribed artistic practices was not merely a walk away from "desecrated art" but a coming into contention with journalism and photojournalsm, thereby approaching greater social centrality. Piscator equated journalism with "the actuality of the day." To Heartfield it was "the history of the moment"—i.e., where "news" makes the present epoch manif est. In *Trotz Alledem!* documentary was brought into play to both depict and convince. What had once existed as journalism had the advantage of being mass (media) vernacular, of being familiar. Unfamiliar material, such as film from WWI, gathered its advantage from being the disclosure of suppressed documents.

As in Heartfield's later photographic work, the play, using film and projections, combined image and text. Textual documentation was also included on placards and within the actors' narrations and dialogue. "The whole performance was a montage of authentic speeches, essays, newspaper cuttings, apppeals, pamphlets, photographs, and film of the War and the Revolution, of historical persons and scenes."

All this provided an "authentic", non-psychological backdrop of political and economic history from which individual action was to evolve, i.e., the action of the characters in the play and ideally the action of the viewers upon leaving the theater. It also provided discrete representations of the SPD, military, bourgeoisie, and working class along poles of ridicule or exhortation, accordingly. Potent critiques could be delivered by presenting incriminatingly contradictory elements—SPD voting for War loans/first dead—or by running commentary upon an invoked image. As with Heartfield's work the compositional arsenal was extensive. The important aspect was the capacity of journalism and photography to render the objects of critique sitting ducks, mute ones at that. If all went well the theatre audience was to leave the with feathers in their teeth, and a song, the Internationale, springing from their lips.

Piscator's work ushered a critical cultural utilization of technology and journalism into mid-Weimar. This affinity had long existed for Heartfield. Even while a Dadaist he had little in common with the Zurich Dadaist Hugo Ball who, while prefacing a sound poetry recitation at the Cabaret Voltaire, stated that in order to save language "devastated by journalism" it was necessary to "retreat into the alchemy of the word", to where literacy was problematic. In his first major ventures of *Neue Jugend* with its "American newspaper format" Heartfield was closer to Karl Kraus who attacked journalism from his own journalistic platform. This attack from the inside is a positioning among social practices most comfortable for the parodist and satirist who, unlike actors, take on roles for the purpose of destroying them. Of course, on a societal scale *Neue Jugend* could not attack from the "inside" since it was localized to Bohemian regions. This was a hindrance to Heartfield's work which would be remedied when he joined a newspaper that had entered a competitive journalistic sphere.

Heartfield's unique position comes from the fact that he was the only Weimarian visual artist within this confluence of journalism and (photographic) technology. Grosz had a fat foot in the door of journalism but by the late-20s, despite earlier photomontages, he developed an antipathy toward its technology. Both Grosz and Heartfield, however, had self-proclaimed precedent prior to the 20th century. "High art, so far as it strove to portray the beauty of the world, was of less interest to me than ever—I was interested in the tendentious painters, the moralists: Hogarth, Goya, Daumier and such artists." (Grosz) After his drawings for Piscator's production of *Good Soldier Schwejk* (a Malik portfolio for which both he and Herzfelde were charged with blasphemy) Grosz encouraged all the "Daumiers of today" to "speak directly to the masses" using the backdrops of stages; he also instructed them to draw with a line that must be "photogenic".

Heartfield knew Daumier's work through Eduard Fuchs, "a friend who had been like a father. . . . It was he more than anyone else who had introduced Germany to the works of the genial French caricaturist and painter."[37] Apart from the particular analogies (and, in fact, some directly incorporated motifs) with Daumier's lithographs, Heartfield's work had in common mass distribution—Daumier's *Caricature* and *Charivari* becoming *Neue Jugend* and *A-I-Z*. Thematically, both brought together the two time frames which Arnold Hauser calls "epochal consciousness", i.e. the moment and the "times". Concerning this, Henry James wrote in article on Daumier: ". . .The very essence of the art of Daumier is to be historical. . . . Many industrious seekers have ascended the stream of time to follow to its source the modern movement of pictorial satire. The stream of time is in this case mainly the stream of journalism; for social and political caricature, as the present century has practiced it, is only journalism made doubly vivid."[38]

Josep Renau, Spanish photomontagist and graphic artist, active

sch auf London

JAHRGANG VIII NR. 8
20 Pf.
15 Kon.
40 Gr.
30 Cent.

A·J·Z

DIE ARBEITER-... IERTE ZEITUNG ALLE... NDER

DAUMIER
...AG DES GROSSEN
...REN ZEICHNERS

DER DEMOKRATISCH-
KAPITALISTISCHE
„WELTFRIEDE"

during the Spanish Civil War, in an article on Heartfield placed him in the pantheon of political satire. He first noted an historical impulse toward documentation in Goya.

> In the last graphic cycles of his life, it is obvious that Goya conscientiously placed his quality as a *witness of the facts* above any other quality of his art. In *The Disasters of War*, an evident documentary zeal places him closer to today's graphic reporters than to the painters of his day. He anxiously attempted to support the *truthfulness* of his images with the plain comments he wrote beneath them: "Unsightly," "Right or Wrong," "Because of a Jackknife," "So it was," "I saw it". . .[39]

However, Renau does not consider photography within specific social practices (especially that photography's status as document glided in on the wings of journalism) when he noted "a brutal and violent discontinuity between Heartfield's art and that of Goya [due to] a *massive irruption* of a new objective factor unprecedented in the millenary development of methods of visual presentation: the photographic image." The objectivity of the photographic image provided the ability "to explain and to resolve problems of a concrete logic for the masses," and could convey "emotional and dramatic values. . . not reached by the traditional means of expression." Thus, "Yesterday Goya. Today John Heartfield." If only Daumier had possessed a "pencil of nature" his journalism would have been triply vivid.

The third "semi-autonomous" institution(s) with which Heartfield was associated were those associated with Willi Münzenberg. Unlike the Malik Verlag or the theater of Piscator, which had established themselves vis-a-vis the party from the bottom-up, Münzenberg came to the KPD from the top-down. Because of a formidable track record in leadership of socialist and communist youth organizations, among other reasons, Münzenberg was personally appointed by Lenin to direct the Internationale Arbeiter Hilfe (Workers International Relief—IAH). After Lenin's death this recognition worked as a patrimonial credit card within the internal communist struggles for a piece of Lenin lineage. The IAH involved him in international activities in which Mother Russia was favored over his own Germany. The same could be said of his position within the Comintern. For these reasons, not to mention the successes rallied from these positions, Münzenberg operated from a relatively "supra-party" position. Thus aided by the Russia-to-Germany party slope, normal organizational friction gave way to momentum of innovation and accomplishment.

IAH's goal was to bring relief to the famine suffered in the Soviet Union and to aid in reconstruction.

> Münzenberg proved to be extremely inventive in devising methods for his relief work: direct appeals were made to foreign parliaments and yielded a half-million kronen from Sweden, one million from Norway, and two million from Denmark; German workers were asked to contribute one or two days' wages, overtime and Sunday wages; workers' relief committees were formed to organize collection meetings, street corner appeals, door-to-door canvassing, sports events, cultural and artistic evenings, theater performances and exhibitions of Russian posters and paintings; sewing centers were started at which workers' wives spent Sundays repairing donated clothing; and collections were made of jewelry and workers' tools and instruments.[40]

A good amount of support was also received from Herbert Hoover's American Relief Administration. The appeals for aid to Russia as well a campaign outside Russia enlisted the legitimizing support of some of the world's most prominent figures: Einstein, Shaw, Gandhi, Romain Rolland, Gorki, Upton Sinclair, and Thomas Mann to name a few. The first IAH pamphlet, which was published in Malik's *Der Gegner, Helft! Russland in Not!* (Help! Russia in Distress!) included contributions by John Reed, Mayakovsky, Kollwitz and Grosz. Münzenberg's ability to enlist support extended to the unlikely terrain of antagonistic political parties, where he brought together the SPD, KPD and USPD (Independent Socialist Party) during early Weimar.

> At its height in 1931 the IAH in Germany comprised 932 local groups with 105,000 members. It included divisions for women, children and youth and provided a host of social services for German workers; bureaus; offering information about state and federal welfare benefits; pediatric clinics; children's homes, nurseries and summer camps; emergency relief stations for striking workers; and campaigns for the repeal of Paragraph 218 of the Penal Code which classified abortion as a felony.

International activities of the IAH during its first decade included: aid to victims of Russian famine; aid to victims of the Japanese earthquake in 1923-24; support of strikes in Shanghai and Canton in 1924; aid to striking English miners in 1926; organization of foreign support of German workers during inflation years; campaigns for the liberation of Matthias Rakosi and Sacco and Vanzetti; and support of strikers in Ireland, Sweden, Norway, Denmark, Iceland, Holland, France, Belgium, Switzerland, Czechoslovakia, India, South Africa, and the United States.

The IAH was only part of Münzenberg's activities. He was a Reichstag deputy from 1924, member of the Comintern, spoke frequently at demonstrations and events, and organized numerous international congresses and campaigns. He was probably best known for constructing a media conglomerate consisting of film production and distribution, a number of daily newspapers, journals, books and pamphlets, and the initiation of the Workers' Photography Leagues and their magazine *Der Arbeiter-Fotograf*. Münzenberg's entrepreneurial streak traveled as far as cigarettes! "One of Münzenberg's last involvements in 1932 was in a Berlin cigarette factory whose owner had pro-Communist leanings. National Socialists had persuaded a Dresden firm to enclose in its brand *The Drummer* [Hitler was known as the Drummer] pictures of Nazi celebrities. Thereupon, the manufacturers of *Solidarity* cigarettes, in which the Neuer Deutscher Verlag [a Munzenberg enterprise] had a share, enclosed pictures of workers' leaders in their packets. Within a few months the sales of *Solidarity* rose considerably and the factory received letters from smoking workers who enthused over *Red Selection* at 2-1/2 pfennig a cigarette, or *Collective* at 3-1/2 pfennig. . ."

Münzenberg's publishing career began when, as secretary of the Socialist Youth International, he edited the organization's journal. In 1919 he authored the first German account of the Russian Revolution and in November 1921 began a series of IAH magazines, the first being *Soviet Russia in Pictures*, an illustrated monthly magazine with a circulation of nearly 100,000. This was followed by *Sickle and Hammer* (circ. 180,000) in 1923 and was accompanied by IAH newspapers *Warning Cry* (bi-monthly, 140,000) and a local version of *Warning Cry* (80,000), and a theoretical journal *Red Construction*.

Toward the end of 1923 the KPD was outlawed as a result of the aborted uprisings at Saxony and Hamburg. The IAH was not among the organizations proscribed because it was not an official organ of the KPD. It could be officially overlooked also because it had been bringing relief to the German working class during the inflation. In 1924, however, Münzenberg decided to set up a publishing concern, Neuer Deutscher Verlag (NDV), separate from the IAH because the IAH was associated too closely with the KPD. Close association jeopardized the stability and continuity of publication if the periodic banning of the Communist main organ *Die Rote Fahne* was any indication. Close association also threatened the desire to reach an audience which was not already comprised of party members. Distance from the KPD was advised, especially after the failures and embarrassments of 1923, even if the goal was an ultimate mediation through the KPD. Distancing from the party did not come easily since the KPD was resistant to tolerating any further competition to its own multitude of publications. It eventually succumbed to Münzenberg's Lenin sanction, IAH successes, etc., and provided much needed initial financial and distributive support for the new NDV publications.

NDV's first publications were heavily influenced by their early party patronage. As its finances improved and markets opened up outside party distribution networks, it began to select its own stable of contributors. In 1925 NDV launched the bi-weekly *Arbeiter Illustrierte*, the forerunner to A-I-Z, which included many non-communist contributors and staff. One gauge of NDV's eventual degree of autonomy was their 1929 publication of *Deutschland, Deutschland über alles*, written by the systematically independent Kurt Tucholsky and illustrated by Heartfield.

Tucholsky was *the* outstanding literary satirist of Weimar, a polemicist and one-time editor of the journal *Die Weltbühne*, the meeting ground for the "left-wing intellectuals". He made his living and reputation from an ability to irreparably cite, indict, and convict from any angle a German society that had gone from "Dichter und Denker" to "Richter und Henker" (from poets and thinkers to judges and executioners). Although he had supported the IAH the KPD did not escape his wit. "KPD? A pity that you are not a member so that you could now be expelled."[41] Similiarly, he neither had respect for the *Cudgel*, the KPD satirical journal co-edited by Heartfield, nor for *Die Rote Fahne*, "Unfortunately, it is not a newspaper." The KPD, however, was for many of the "left-wing intellectuals" a guaranteed conduit to the working class from which they, despite their desires, were sorely divorced. They looked upon Münzenberg as the most reasonable among the calcified upper party ranks. He had a history of placing many non-party members on his staffs and even had non-party editors of his publications. Such positions, however, were contingent upon certain adherences vacillating between independent thought and party centralism, of uncritical stances toward the KPD, Comintern and Soviet Union. Consequently, it was definitely a question of compromise for someone like Tucholsky to meet the KPD, or anyone, half-way. Münzenberg's wife Babette Gross recalls that, "Tucholsky distrusted the militant and orthodox world of the Communist Party. But John Heartfield and I went calling on him until we finally presuaded him to change his mind."

They persuaded him to collaborate with Heartfield on the NDV book *Deutschland, Deutschland über alles*. This put Tucholsky's relationship with the Ullstein newspaper chain into jeopardy. He let them know, however, that if they continued to have problems with his planned NDV book he'd rather leave Ullstein. He didn't leave and *Deutschland* became somewhat of a centerpiece for Tucholsky's Weimar public profile, selling nearly 50,000 copies within a year of its July 1929 release.

The book, named after "a really bad poem which a really demented Republic chose for its national anthem," contained a photomontage that Heartfield included at the last minute which created quite a stir. It showed eight retired Teutonic militaroids with the caption "Animals looking at you," aping, so to speak, an animal picture book popular the previous year. When asked to comment on this photomontage Tucholsky answered that he wasn't wild about it since "insulting animals is not my taste."

This exhumed, good-ol'-boy mentality was the target of the cover; a plump-jowled, flag-striped head wearing a Prussian helmet covered by top hat. It sported half-military attire, half-capitalist attire with a "Pour le Meritè" medallion. From a lipless gaping abyss where a mouth should be the head sings the title of the book. This proved to be controversial also for the "financial paper of the German book trade refused to advertise the book because of John Heartfield's photomontage on the cover."[42]

Animals looking at you

Kurt Tucholsky

Deutschland Deutschland über alles

Under its anthem Germany presented itself a sappy collaborationist whole, a "brotherly sticking together" as the song instructs a parallel society oddly voided of women and classes. If there was a semblance of order it was achieved in the manner Heartfield depicted on the back cover, a raised police truncheon flanked by a military saber being pulled from its sheath. The order gratuitously bestowed by the state shrouded, like a polished symptoma, a body politic "as inharmonious as a slag heap," shrapnel still reverberating from the war. "Germany looks like a battlefield on which dismembered hands, legs, arms and other parts lie scattered, while the blood of life runs forgotten into the sand."

Tucholsky sought to splay Germany to open it up to surgical view, showing the connections between, say, Stresemann and mailbox design or bureaucracy and little button eyes. This was not a pretty sight, no culinary exercise to use Brecht's term. Nor was it an "official cross-section" since they "always cut the cheese without hitting the maggots. We wanted to do it differently. Whatever you see moving as you cut, is a maggot. And part of Germany."

In this collaboration, Heartfield met Tucholsky on Tucholsky's satirical turf, one more atuned to daily life and more occupied with generalizing socio-psychological traits through corporeal means. Heartfield had already been by 1928 at least aspiring toward more analytical cogency than "An ass with ears," despite any marked resemblance with persons past or present. However, the expertise with which Tucholsky often edged in on the intricacies of politics embedded in daily life remained almost entirely foreign to Heartfield. The book collaboration did, nevertheless, give Heartfield an appetite for longer texts and more complex interactions with text and image, although most of the images he supplied to Tucholsky's texts were not composite.

After this venture, Heartfield started collaborating on another NDV publication, one with which he has become equated, the *Arbeiter Illustrierte Zeitung*, the Worker's Illustrated Paper.

From its ancient beginnings in the casting of coinage, the mass reproduction of imagery, text and other exchangables reached, during Weimar, the level of inundation—the din we take today for the lay of the land. "The five years after WWI was Germany's

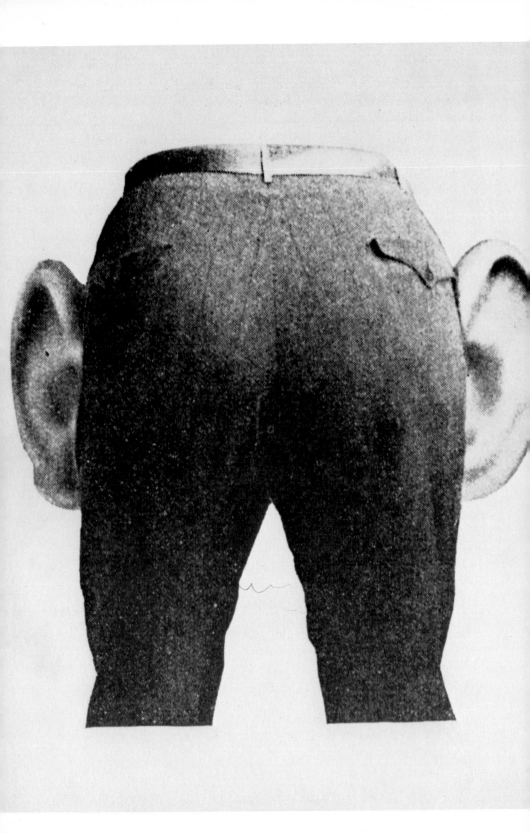

Paper Age. Early every morning the banknotes littering the street were carried away by the cartload along with the rest of the waste-paper. . ."[43]

Once the inflation, which made banknotes worth less than the paper they were printed upon, eased up (by a complex of measures including the printing of new currency in November 1923) Germany's Paper Age proceeded unfettered.

> Locust swarms of print, which already eclipse the sun of what is taken for the intellect for city dwellers, will grow thicker with each succeeding year.[44]

Photographic and printing technologies which already had been available coalesced in the latter half of the 20s in a plethora of practices and products. Photography ran the whole gamut: scientific and medical, architectural and city planning, industrial and product design, advertising and publicity, art and art photography. Its marked increase ruptured previous photo milieus, institutions and discourses, creating hybrid forms which filled the stores, streets, books, press agencies, magazines, galleries, libraries, archives, and other rummaging sites of Heartfield.

Where the new developments in photography met those of the printing press stood Weimar's illustrated newspapers, vehicles for high resolution photojournalism and photoreportage. These large format, rotogravure weeklies became the premiere forms of German mass media. For Americans they were finally registered in the 1930s in the form of the confidently named magazine *Life*.

The largest of the illustrated papers, the *Berliner Illustrietre Zeitung* (BIZ), was published by the mammoth Ullstein enterprise whose flagship publication *Vossische Zeitung—Auntie Voss—*was the *New York Times* of the day. At its peak in the early 30s BIZ had a circulation around two million. It maintained a liberal stance until late Weimar when it compliantly moved right. Ullstein's reporting staff regularly, and under full knowledge of Ullstein, submitted items to the German Socialist News Agency in hope of vitalizing the dreary socialist press throughout Europe. Many of these individuals left Ullstein when it abandoned its campaign against capital punishment, its cooperative stance toward Russia and its support for abortion and homosexual law reform etc., leaving these and other concerns for the Communist and "fellow-travelling" press.

Vender of bourgeois illustrated papers, all showing cover image of Hindenburg

Weimar journalistic writing regularly forefronted the politics of a paper, at times graphically forefronted by running editorials on the front page. The phenomenon was compounded by by the publications of the political parties (the 1932 ballot listed no less than 27), in addition to the political affiliations of the independent press ownership. One prominent example was media magnate Alfred Hugenberg. An ex-Krupp munitions executive and leader in the late-20s of the ultra-conservative Deutschenationale Volkspartei, he reigned over 150 newspapers as well as Germany's major film production company UFA. He was indispensible to the rise of Hitler when, after their mutual opposition to the Young Plan, his newspapers began announcing Nazi meetings and rallies. The Nazis and their press had up to that point been adequately marginalized.

Within the political heat of journalism, photojournalism appeared cooly confident. This was a time when photographs were not read and passed over so quickly; they were the fascinating apparitions anchoring a still consolidating application of urban technology, a mental industrialism. The detachment which they achieved can be attributed to a great degree to the consistent flow of inaugural appearances. The smaller, more mobile cameras, quicker films and lenses, plus higher resolution printing processes, made available to a mass audience hitherto uncharted reaches of social reality. It was a terrain littered with photographic "objects" unsubjected to the disembodied scrutiny of millions. Monasteries and other inner sanctums were disrobed. The technologies and practices also afforded an unexplored nuancing of gesture and texture. This offered up still more photographic objects as well as recycling the more familiar, staid photographs which, through repetition, threatened to sink into format. For example, the bust of Gustav Stresemann could now be seen at the beach, in important meetings which Erich Salomon attended with his clandestine camera, or imperceptibly wrinkling the lower-lids which cupped his protruding eyeballs. The call for detailing of both movement and surface, the demands of speeding minutia and fleeting novelty, were answered by an onslaught of new photographers equipped with their ready expertise, often after having migrated from other professions.

All this was part of a "mighty recasting" of socio-cultural distinctions operating during the Weimar Republic, of which Walter Benjamin spoke in his article "Author as Producer," a recasting of "conventional distinctions between genres, between writer and poet, between scholar and popularizer. . . between author and reader." Unlike the Soviet Union which was also going through a recasting, the undisturbed class structures in the capitalist nations directed the new possibilities toward an ideological disorganization of the working class and a *de facto* organization of the ruling class. This was epitomized by the bourgeois newspapers' "theater of confusion." The confusion was exacerbated in the illustrated magazine with its attractive photography which metallically vaporized all connectedness into its own silver society.

The illustrated papers met with early criticism; Siegfried Kracauer in an article in the *Frankfurter Zeitung*, 10 October 1927, wrote:

> In illustrated magazines, the public sees the world whose reality illustrated magazines prevent them from perceiving. . . There never was an era which was so ill-informed about itself. The device of the illustrated magazine in the hands of the ruling society has become one of the most powerful means of striking against the spread of knowledge. The successful implementation of this strike is helped by the jumbled arrangement of the pictures. The arbitrary way in which they have been placed side by side systematically precludes the connection which stimulates consciousness. The picture idea ousts the real idea; the photographic snowstorm reveals the indifference to what the photographed objects were meant to convey.

Similar sentiment was echoed by Bertolt Brecht in 1931:

> The tremendous development of photojournalism has contributed practically nothing to the revelation of the truth about the conditions in this world. On the contrary, photography, in the hands of the bourgeoisie, has become a terrible weapon against the truth. The vast amount of pictured material that is being disgorged daily by the press and that seems to have the character of truth serves in reality only to obscure the facts. The camera is just as capable of lying as the typewriter. The task of A-I-Z, which is to restore the truth, is of paramount importance under these circumstances and it seems to me that it fulfills this purpose extremely well.

This statement appeared in A-I-Z's pages and was made on the occasion of its 10th anniversary. It had been ten years since the

IAH monthly *Sowjetrussland im Bild*. Through IAH's *Sichel und Hammer* and NDV's *Arbeiter Illustrierte*, A-I-Z appeared weekly in 1927. According to its own figures it had a circulation of nearly a quarter million in 1927 doubling to 500,000 in the early thirties, but according to Karl Retzlaw, who worked in NDV circulation, the figure never topped 280,000. These figures would have to be compared with the *Berliner Illustrierte* 1928 circulation of 1.6 million and 500,000 for *Münchner Illustrierte Presse* (edited by Stefan Lorant, later editor of England's *Llliput* and *Picture Post*), with *BIZ* increasing to over two million in the early 30s (I couldn't find a figure for *MIP*). A-I-Z in the early 30s, when Heartfield's work began appearing regularly, was solidly within a competitive journalistic realm, especially if the collective reading habits of its less affluent readership are taken into account. In 1929 A-I-Z reported its readership as: 42% skilled workers, 33% unskilled, 10% clerks, 5% youth, 3.5% housewives, 3% professionals, 2% self-employed, 1% civil servants. Although their distribution outside Germany was concentrated in the German speaking regions of Austria, Czechslovakia and Switzerland, it did reach out to the world's four corners of Vancouver, Montevideo, Sidney and Tokyo.

A typical issue would include, in remarkably innovative layout, photojournalistic pieces on domestic and international affairs and conditions; "human interest" spreads; a serialized novel; poetry; a women's page (mostly fashion and household hints) or a children's page (equally as enlightened); a page of jokes, cartoon, and crossword puzzle (where many of the words referred to political history); very little advertising except for communist publications and tours to the Soviet Union, although in the later 30s there were occasional pages filled with shoes; and a full or double-page artwork. The latter was usually produced by Heartfield throughout the 30s but there were also appearances by Tina Modotti, Käthe Kollwitz, and an artist whose muddled derivations of Kollwitz are probably less remembered than his/her name—Fuck.

One very famous 1931 story in A-I-Z presented the life of a Russian family named "The Filipovs." It followed the family through their daily life to show the improved living conditions within the Soviet Union during a time of economic collapse in the West. It had such currency, ten weeks after the story first ran a group of

KRUPP UND THYSSEN
»KURBELN AN!«

Dieselben Wirtschaftsführer, die Krupp, Thyssen, Vögler, die im Dritten Reich die Markabwertung fordern, haben schon einmal durch ein Währungsmanöver riesige Profite eingeheimst: durch die Inflation vor zehn Jahren. Inflation — was war das, was heißt das? Nichts anderes als Geldentwertung durch schrankenlosen Notendruck, durch hemmungslose Produktion von Papiernoten, deren Entwertung im gleichen Maße wächst wie ihre Umfangsmenge. Die Lohn- und Gehaltsempfänger wurden völlig ausgepowert. Hunderttausende Mittelständler ruiniert, nur das Finanzkapital und die Großindustrie bereicherten sich bei diesem Raubzug.

Die neue „Arbeitsschlacht" des Dritten Reichs hat begonnen — mit viel Tamtam, aber doch gedämpfter in Szene gesetzt, als ihre letztjährige Vorgängerin, deren Resultate mehr als mager sind. Zur gleichen Zeit, da die „Arbeitsschlacht" beginnt, zeigen sich am wirtschaftlichen Horizont des Dritten Reiches neue Sturmzeichen. Die Golddeckung der Mark beträgt nunmehr 8%, die Bestände der Reichsbank an ausländischen Devisen schmelzen wie Schnee in der Sonne, die Handelsbilanz ist (seit sieben Jahren zum erstenmal) passiv. Das mußte so kommen, denn die Ausfuhr hat in diesem einen Jahr nationalsozialistischer Herrschaft einen Tiefstand sondergleichen erreicht, während die Einfuhr gleichzeitig stieg. Steigende Einfuhr könnte das Zeichen einer Wirtschaftsbelebung sein. Und so versucht es die gleichgeschaltete Presse auch darzustellen. Aber die gesteigerte Einfuhr des Dritten Reichs wird nicht durch die Kaufkraft der breiten Bevölkerungskreise bewirkt. Nein, die Einfuhrsteigerung hat andere Ursachen. Man führt in erhöhtem Maße Rohstoffe ein: erstens für die Rüstungsindustrie und zweitens für die künstlich angekurbelte Arbeitsbeschaffung. Hier wie dort wird nicht für einen gesteigerten Bedarf gearbeitet, sondern auf Lager. Und wo die Arbeitsbeschaffung nicht zur Überfüllung schon voller Lager dient, dort dient die „Ankurbelung" unproduktiven Zwecken. So erhält beispielsweise die solinger Stahlindustrie Riesenaufträge für SA-Dolche. Pforzheim wird mit der Herstellung von Festabzeichen der Arbeitsfront beschäftigt. Und Plauen wird durch Bestellung von Hakenkreuzrosetten „belebt". All das belastet natürlich den Staatshaushalt, geht auf Kosten der Steuerzahler, ist Raubbau.

Wie wenig von einer steigenden Kaufkraft der Massen gesprochen werden kann, zeigt die Tatsache, daß trotz allen Neueinstellungen (die als Erfolge der „Arbeitsschlacht" gebucht werden) die Gesamtsumme nicht steigt, sondern gefallen ist und fällt!

Was nun aber bei passiver Handelsbilanz, bei schmelzenden Gold- und Devisenvorräten tun? Die Einfuhr drosseln, das hieße die Rüstungen einschränken und das Arbeitsprogramm ganz und gar preisgeben. Gewiß, man wird — wie es schon im Vorjahre geschah — die ohnehin nicht imposanten Aufwendungen für die Arbeitsbeschaffung kürzen. Aber das schließt noch nicht die „Schere" zwischen gesunkener Ausfuhr und gestiegener Einfuhr, umsoweniger, als eingeführte Rohstoffe infolge der „Rüstungskonjunktur" zur Zeit in die Höhe klettern, während die Preise für Fertigwaren auf dem Weltmarkt sinken oder durch Dumping gesenkt werden. Also muß die Ausfuhr gehoben werden. Aber wie? Gewiß, man wird die Löhne abbauen, aber direkte Lohnsenkungen steigern die ohnehin schon wachsende Erbitterung und Enttäuschung. Bleibt also die Abwertung der Mark. Die Großindu-

„Abwertung, dirigierte Entwertu... „Devalvation" heißt das Heilmi... das die Schere zwischen der gesu... nen Ausfuhr und der gestiegenen ... fuhr des Dritten Reichs schli... soll. Aber was als „geregelte, ... lige Abwertung der Mark" beg... wird angesichts der zerrütteten W... schaftslage des Dritten Reichs a... anders enden.

strie rechnet damit, daß dadu... der Export gehoben, die Dros... lung der Einfuhr, der Stillste... der Rüstungen und das Auffle... men großer Lohnkämpfe ver... den wird. Denn es sinkt ja ... der Reallohn und die Krupp ... Thyssen, die Ley und Feder n... men an, daß der Arbeiter ... nicht merken wird. Natürlich ... diese Rechnung falsch. Die V... schaft des Dritten Reichs ist ... zerrüttet, daß sich eine Abw... wertung nicht einfach „komm... dieren" und „dirigieren" l... Der Export wird infolge der H... delskriege, die das Dritte R... allenthalben entfesselt, nicht s... gen. Die Arbeitsschlacht wird ... wenig Erfolg haben wie bis... Und die Enttäuschung, Erbitter... der breiten Massen wird im g... chen Maße wachsen wie ... Not. Aber die Großindustrie, ...

Die neue „Arbeitsschlacht" wurde mit einer Hitlerrede in Unteraching eröffnet. Sie galt den Arbeiter... auf einer der strategischen Autobahnen. Die Erwerbslosen, die beim Bau dieser Bahnen, bei anderen ... stungsbauten, in den Werften und Rüstungsbetrieben „neu eingestellt" werden, sind Zwangsarbeiter, ... anderen. Ihr Lohn bleibt unter der früheren Arbeitslosenunterstützung

worker photographers produced "The German Filipovs." The problem with the original story was that in selecting one family as representative it glossed over those Russian families subject to the growing brutalities of forced collectivization and those whose lives were not as casually harmonious as the Filipovs'. Babette Gross recalls in her memoirs of Münzenberg that "Senior Russian officials were sarcastic among themselves about the Filipov serial. Such blatant propaganda annoyed them and the saying 'as at the Filipovs' became their synonym for Potemkin villages." (The term "Potemkin villages" derives from the sham, prosperous villages on the banks of the Dnieper in the Crimea reportedly constructed in early 1787 with lath and plaster, peasants and cattle, by General Potemkin especially for the benefit and/or deception of Catherine the Great and her opulent river entourage.)

Uncritical embraces of the Soviet Union by German Communists were often undermined by Russian duplicity toward Germany as a whole, as in the case of KPD anti-militarism. The SPD was sharing power in one of Weimar's "Great Coalitions" with the German People's Party, German Democratic Party and the Catholic Center Party. During the election of 1928, one of the SPD's campaign slogans was "Pocket battleship or feeding centers for children?" A pocket battleship was one which complied with Versailles Treaty limitations on size but was nevertheless a decided move toward remilitarization. Immediately following the elections, however, the other parties demanded funding for the battleship under threat of dissolving the coalition. The SPD acquiesced. Heartfield was working at the center of the KPD with its main organ *Die Rote Fahne*.

> *Die Rote Fahne* things went more or less like this: We would say, "My dear Johnny, we will be coming out next Sunday and we want to print a page of a particular sort. . ." e.g., against the new pocket battleships of the Weimar Republic. . . He then would propose his idea, it was discussed, it was approved, perhaps with some suggestion to make it more complete. It was discussed, naturally, but the idea had to come from the artist himself, it was not given to him by anyone. —Alexander Abusch, Chief Editor, *DRF*.[45]

The revelations at the end of 1926 that the Reichswehr was receiving military armaments and training from the Soviet Union

1931 demonstration on a beach against pocket battleships

should have given rise to hesitations within the working process outlined by Abusch. The degree of autonomy of the artist vis-a-vis the newspaper was not similarly applied to the subject matter.

Heartfield visited Moscow and was photographed at a table with the Filipovs. It was published in NDV's *Magazin für Alle* to evidence, contrary to accusations printed in *Vorwärts*, that the Filipovs existed and maintained the existence attributed to them in the A-I-Z reportage. The person who had assumed a public profile by bringing photographic credibility into question was the one whose attendance brought credibility to a photograph of the Filipovs. He sat at the table showing the family the A-I-Z issue which pictured them on the cover. Noticably absent from the table top was a pair of scissors.

By 1931, Heartfield's work was known well enough that by cutting up it began to undercut precepts of photographs appearing in the illustrated magazines. Any photograph appearing in their pages could be entertained as being the future or past object of Heartfield's anonymous machinations, i.e., while disclosing the hidden reality of some photographs he hid himself. This was felt

AIZ

Erscheint wöchentlich ... 1.60 Kč, 30 Gr., 1.25 Frs., 30 Rp. ... einzelnummer ... Cr. 15 ... Co. ... Jahrgang XII. · Nr. 36. · 14. September 1933

CHEN VOLKE

GOERING
DER HENKER
DES DRITTEN REICHS

Pour le Pro fit

In Leipzig werden am 21. September neben
dem Provokateur Lubbe, vier Unschuldige
— Opfer eines der ungeheuerlichsten Justizver-
rechen — vor Gericht stehen. Der wahre
Reichstagsbrandstifter, Goering, wird nicht vor
den Schranken erscheinen.

Fotomontage: John Heartfield // Umschlagbild des „Braunbuchs über Reichstagsbrand und Hitlerterror" // Das Gesicht Goerings ist einer Originalfotografie entnommen und wurde nicht retuschiert.

SONDERNUMMER · REICHSTAGSBRAND   PROZES GEGENPRO

several times in A-I-Z issues where full page photographic covers which, because of their self-incriminating or idiosynchratic character, had to be ·accompanied with a note saying they were un-manipulated. The phenomenon even creeped back into one of Heartfield's photomontages, "Goering, The Executioner of the Third Reich", upon which it was noted that "Goering's face comes from an actual photograph and has not been retouched." This disruption of photographic images, even a residual disruption where not intended, falls within tactics prescribed by Kracauer, continuing his critique of illustrated magazines quoted above.

> In order for the subject to be meaningfully represented, the mere surfaces offered by the photograph must somehow be disrupted. . . the likeness achieved by the photograph refers only to the exterior of the object, which does not readily disclose its internal meaning as it manifests itself to the understanding.

The type of disruption proposed here may seem similar to cubism. It is significant that it recapitulates the scenario enacted within art against the pictorial space which photography inherited. Only here, within Kracauer's 1927 prescription, it is lodged against the most advanced form of mass media. Heartfield worked from both inside and outside, taking such a prescription literally, that is to say, materially, physically disrupting the photograph proper as well as usurping the usurpative functions of an editor in cropping, captioning and placing a photograph in relation to a specific text and to other photographs. In his utilization of all aspects and processes of an illustrated magazine, i.e., text, image and editing, he was in a position to embody a critique of the form and practice, from a competitive platform where the critique could be observed. Institutionally, Heartfield "recasted" the roles of photographer, journalist and editor, coming from two practices which were not inherent in ilustrated magazines, avant-garde art and revolutionary communist politics, generally bringing a critique of form from the former and a critique of history from the latter.

THE TIGER MONTAGE

What German worker does not know this one or that photomontage
by Heartfield—the "cabbbagetop," the elegant gentleman with
stand-up collar and tiger head, . . . or the arrest of Karl Marx by the
former Berlin chief of police Zörgiebel? All these pictures have
appeared in A-I-Z, illustrated weekly of the German proletariat.
                                                    —Alfred Durus, 1934.

The most dangerous doctors are those born actors who imitate born
doctors with perfect deceptive art.
                                                    —Friedrich Nietzsche

Heartfield formally entered competitive journalistic realms with a
full page photomontage in the 9 February 1930 issue of A-I-Z. The
photomontage showed a head fishwrapped (cabbagetop) in two
newspapers, *Tempo* and *Vorwärts*, captioned "Those who read
bourgeois newspapers will become blind and deaf." A critique of
journalism *per se* was not the pre-eminent concern. Both newspapers were organs of the SPD.

This was not an isolated attack on the SPD. Of the dozen photomontages for A-I-Z in 1930 eight contained attacks of one form or
another, in 1931 three of four did so, after 1931 only around half-
a-dozen. When compared to the nearly 250 photomontages he
produced for A-I-Z the total number of attacks on the Socialists
may seem proportionally insignificant. Such proportions, however, mean little for an artist who created works for the "history of

the moment." It is not insignificant that the greater number of his attacks on the SPD came during the last years of the Weimar Republic, before Hitler took over at the end of January 1933. Of these one will be discussed in depth; the 15 June 1931 photomontage "The Crisis Party Congress of the SPD," referred to hereafter as the "Tiger montage." It is one of Heartfield's best-remembered works, probably because of its potent affectivity. As it was remembered in late-Weimar the photomontage's affectivity existed within a heated, albeit cool and direct sphere of political contestation. As it is remembered now, the politics have dropped away, not just the politics of the specific moment, of the historical conjuncture, but nearly all political references. The discussion here is not a representative analysis of the "workings" of Heartfield's mature photomontages. Photography plays a lesser role and the journalistic text is relied upon more distinctly than other late-Weimar photomontages. The purpose is to show how, in a cultural practice of political primacy, a "powerful" photomontage can be a political mistake and thus a failure as a photomontage.

Because of a visit to the Soviet Union Heartfield produced only four photomontages for A-I-Z in 1931. The first was "Fraternal Greetings from the SPD", a collage of *Vorwärts* clippings framing the corpse of Karl Liebknecht. The second was the Tiger montage. The third, "Black or White: In Struggle United", was produced for a special issue on race and class which included a feature on the Scottsboro Boys in Alabama. The fourth, like the Tiger montage, arose from the SPD's party congress in Leipzig. It shows SPD Berlin police president Karl Zörgiebel who, on 1 May 1929, had led a brutal attack against Communist demonstrators, killing twenty-five. He has donned a police helmet to personally direct the arrest of Karl Marx, who, with a copy of *Die Rote Fahne* under his arm, looks wryly to the reader for comment. The text reads:

> title: The Latest Wisdom of the SPD: "Down with Marxism!"
> quote: When Karl Marx more than 80 years ago coined the expression that the workers have only their chains to lose, it was a revolutionary act. Now, if the present is to be taken into account, it is an utterly reactionary phrase! (Sollman-Köln at the Leipzig Congress)
> caption: You are arrested as a false prophet, Herr Karl Marx: we have not only our chains to lose, but our cushy posts and comfortable ministerial seats.

Karl Marx vor mehr als 80 Jahren das Wort prägte, daß die Arbeiter nichts zu verlieren hätten als ihre Ketten, war es eine revolutionäre Tat.
ist es, wenn es für die Gegenwart nachgebetet wird, **eine stockreaktionäre Phrase!** (Sollmann · Köln auf dem Leipziger SPD-Parteitag)

Fotomontage: JOHN HEARTFIELD

e sind verhaftet als falscher Prophet, Herr Karl Marx — wir haben
ht unsere Ketten zu verlieren, sondern unsere Futterkrippen und Ministersessel

Zörgiebel's presence within the photomontage was meant to signal the continuity of SPD repression going back past 1929 in the personage of a latter-day Noske and thus to restore meat and bone to the sanitization which accompanies repressive policy. However, he is distanced from the origins of his reputation in violence and bloodshed as he tamely administers a social democratic act of Marxist heresy and yet further removed by subsumption in a context determined by a satiric rendering of the quote from the Congress. This has a dual consequence of interfering in the photomontage's consistency of statement and, more importantly, supplying Zörgiebel a reprieve through light-heartedness. The urge to connect the SPD Congress with violence in this photomontage came from the successful connection three weeks earlier in the Tiger montage. Formulaic failures require a prior success.

Attacks on the SPD by the Communists proliferated during this period. Sustained polemics, however, were for the most part reserved for the KPD party press, *Die Rote Fahne* or Münzenberg's daily papers. The Tiger montage was the only instance within the issue of A-I-Z in which it appeared. The issue was typical in most respects to other A-I-Z issues in late-Weimar. It covered a wide range of topics, from an article on beatings by Nazis to "When Mother Isn't Home" (the kids get mischievous). The cover showed a young woman in a swimsuit yanking her foot from the water, a crab clamped onto her toe— "Better than being bitten by the stork"(?). Page two carried a photograph of the Scottsboro Boys in the "Pictures of the Week" while, toward the back of the issue, the final frame of the "Felix the Cat" cartoon showed two black monkeys on the roof of Felix's house spitting out watermellon seeds; before this discovery Felix had thought it was raining.

The issue was loaded with photographs and laid out quite dynamically throughout except for the page facing the Tiger montage, which was taken up by the second page text of a serialized novel on stenographers and a small photo of Hitler youth over a poem by Erich Weinert (the cabaret poet and founding editor of the communist literary journal *Linkskurve*). In other words, the Tiger montage had little visual competition, the least in the whole issue. In this way it was framed.

The three components of text in the Tiger montage read in descending order:

A · I · Z

JAHRGANG X
Nr. 24   1931
Preis:
20 Pfg., Kc. 1.60,
30 Gr.   V. b. b.

Neuer Deutscher
Verlag / Berlin W 8

*...besser als
vom Storch gebissen!*

title: The Crisis Party Congress of the SPD
first quotation: "Social Democracy does not want the collapse of capitalism. Like a doctor it wants to heal and improve it." (Fritz Tarnow, Chairman of the Woodworkers Federation)
second quotation: The Veterinarians of Leipzig: "It goes without saying that we shall knock out the teeth of the tiger, but first of all we must feed him and nurse him back to health."

The Crisis Party Congress

The SPD Congress held in Leipzig in May and June 1931 was indeed a "crisis congress", a crisis in party policy amid an unprecedented socio-economic crisis. A fragile Weimar prosperity buttressed by foreign loans, facing years of war reparations, had collapsed as the shock waves of the Great Depression pummeled Germany. The demands on state coffers for unemployment relief led to the dissolution of the last Socialist-led Great Coalition. Governmental control was relinquished to the Center Party's Heinrich Brüning who invoked the "emergency decree" using Article 48 of the constitution. Use of the decree effectively ended parliamentary rule in Weimar, permitting Brüning to rule by "constitutional dictatorship" (the topic of Heartfield's 18 October 1930 photomontage "The Dead Parliament"). The main parties in opposition to the SPD were on the rise as was dissent within its own ranks. They were a party out of control of the republic they had constructed and of which they were still held responsible. However, of all the problems facing ". . . the Social Democrats, fear of a Nazi victory now overrode all other political considerations. . . they reluctantly *tolerated* the Brüning dictatorship as a lesser evil, declining to vote no confidence lest Brüning's fall bring Hitler's ascent."[46]

Toleration was the realpolitik middleground between open support and open attack, a platform for paralysis in a situation calling for definitive action. Action would have required the mobilization of its working class base against both the self-defined requirements of capital-in-crisis and against the Nazis. However, the SPD's picture book reformism was tenured only in the mobilization of its base into the ranks of disciplined and reliant labor; radical politicization let alone a mobilization bridging upon revolution was alien territory.

Throughout Weimar the SPD had maintained an irreconcilable position of being identificatory Marxists and functional monopolists—a classical tightwire act of a transition to socialism gradually evolving out of an advanced development of capitalism. This perpetual state of promise, a socialism for each generation's grandkids, was lockstitched into the constitution and was dependent upon not only a loose-leashed development of capital but also the promise of a progressing democratization from capital. That capitalism was now globally disintegrating and taking its instinctual migration to the authoritarian right, compounded the reformists' dilemma, stretching their tightwire act out to a performance upon a filament.

It was on this suture that Fritz Tarnow, SPD Reichstag Deputy and Chairman of the Woodworkers Federation, had to traipse. In his keynote address to the Leipzig Congress he provided justification for toleration.

> Do we stand at the sickbed of capitalism merely as the diagnostician, or also as the doctor who seeks to cure? Or as joyous heirs, who can hardly wait for the end and would even like to help it along with poison? It seems to me that we are condemned both to be the doctor who earnestly seeks to cure and at the same time to retain the feeling that we are the heirs, who would prefer to take over the entire heritage of the capitalist system today rather than tomorrow.[47]

Anti-Conjuncture

Heartfield based the Tiger montage upon this portion of Tarnow's widely reproduced speech. He excluded the metaphor of heirs/heritage, taking up the cluster of medicine—sickbed, diagnostician, doctor, cure—and the SPD's affirmed position vis-á-vis capital. In the image, capital becomes represented by a tiger and medicine consequently becomes veterinary medicine. There is a further level at which selection and transformation takes place which is more significant.

Tarnow's speech, as the SPD's response to an historically specific moment, spanned a referential range from the *conjunctural* real politik of tolerating the Brüning government to an *epochal*

Zum Krisen-Parteitag der SPD

Sozialdemokratie will nicht den Zusammenbruch des Kapitalismus. Sie will wie ein Arzt heilen und zu bessern versuchen (Fritz Tarnow, Vorsitzender des Holzarbeiterverbandes)

FOTO-MONTAGE: JOHN HE

Die Tierärzte von Leipzig: „Selbstverständlich werden wir dem Tiger die Z usbrechen, aber zunächst einmal müssen wir ihn gesundpflegen und herausfütt

rationalization based upon their ostensibly desired supercession of capital. On this level, Heartfield effectively excludes the former, uniformly favoring the latter. It is with this act that the photomontage may be assessed since every element of the photomontage is informed by it. Even the seemingly arbitrary inclusion of the swastika stickpin makes sense within an epochal framework.

Heartfield's strength resided in his willingess to bring systemic and epochal considerations to bear upon singular events, i.e, to historicize the object. However, when, in this case, the conjunctural (the element predicated by journalism) is not integrated then history loses its moment of enactment and therefore cannot be concretely acted upon.

In the Tiger montage, Heartfield acknowledges conjuncture through the "newsworthy" occasion of the Congress as represented by Tarnow's speech. However, the acknowledgement is minimal. The speech, although addressing a specific moment, coursed along an epochal scale inviting Heartfield to skirt aspects of realpolitik from the beginning. He made good on this invitation by the manner in which he paraphrased the speech. Most importantly he rendered the substance to express a resolve contrary to the speech's actual ambivalence. However, a sense or, rather, a surrogate ambivalence (crisis, dilemma) was preserved by displacing it upon apparently contradictory identifications within the photomontage.

He first set up correspondences between (1) Tarnow/SPD and (2) capitalism/tiger through a continuity in the quotes.

1. Though both quotes are from Tarnow only the first is attributed to him. The second quote is attributed to the "Veterinarians of Leipzig" who, as is evident from the "Leipzig" in the title, are the Social Democrats. The quotes diverge in attribution but are underscored by the same medical metaphor: a doctor treating capitalism, veterinarians treating a tiger (quite exotic when compared to a vet's normal caseload but then again this is no normally exotic tiger). They are also connected by the speech of the SPD: in the first quote through Tarnow speaking for the SPD—"Social Democracy does not want. . ."—and the SPD vets speaking for themselves in the second quote.
2. Capitalism and the tiger are connected in the quotes in that they are the ones receiving medical attention.

In the image of the tiger all four elements are congealed.

1. The tiger seems to be in perfect health and has thus superceded the medical concerns running through the quotes. It has recovered completely from an interspecies head transplant and has accepted the host trunk without complications. It has carried the residual medical connection with capitalism and donned another connection with its formal attire. Although the photomontage arose from the text of the speech at the Congress, the image has, because of its size, centrality, and affectivity, become the cohesive element of the photomontage.
2. Tarnow resides within the tiger through the singularity of the image (all the veterinarians cannot be contained): his speech breaking forth from the muzzle. However, as noted below, his personal role is diminished to a role of agency.
3. The SPD is represented firstly through the occasion of the Congress as indicated by the title hanging over the tiger's head and secondly through the Tarnow/SPD connections.

Contradictory identifications occur as a result of the divergent bases in the quotes and the image. In the quotes Tarnow and the Veterinarians prescribe treatment for capitalism and the tiger, respectively, but in the image they have become the tiger of capitalism; an animal, moreover, which in the entirety of the photomontage is witnessed prescribing its own treatment in the third person. This schizoid identity invokes the sense of (or surrogate) ambivalence but at the same time it circumscribes it as hypocrytical resolve: the malady they are seeking to cure is of their own making, they are their own patient. By trying to "heal and improve" capitalism and "nurse him back to health" they are seeking to insure their own survival, presumably in order to precipitate another crisis.

Heartfield consciously de-emphasizes Tarnow's role in the photomontage. It would have been quite easy to have granted him a predominance but he is held in check.

1. The typographic point size of the quote attributed to him is the smallest among the three bodies of text.
2. His name is cordoned off in parentheses at the end of the quote as opposed to the depersonalized Veterinarians who precede their quote and do so in larger typeface than the words that follow.
3. The second quote from Tarnow is attributed to the SPD as a whole.

4. The tiger face eradicates any possible reference to Tarnow's face. Although this may have to do with the (lack of) currency of his face within the mass media his key(note) role at the Congress and the Party could have been understood to present sufficient impetus to begin to have his face gain recognition, something a Heartfield photomontage, reaching thousands of readers, could go a long way in providing. The superimposition of the tiger's face also needn't have eradicated Tarnow's features. Heartfield's July 1928 "The Face of Fascism" photomontage for the KPD publication *Italy in Chains* fitted Mussolini with exoskeletal facial features while maintaining his recognizability. By not having an image resembling one which will occur in the photographic press the residuary "half-life" function of Heartfield's parodic-photojournalism is left unutilized. In other words, a future encounter in the bourgeois illustrated magazines of a photograph of Tarnow would not invoke memory of a Heartfield parody of *photographs of Tarnow*, nor would it be likely to piggy-back any satiric, critical or informational components. Furthermore, it would be unlikely that an enounter with a photograph of a tiger would prompt a cogent and timely critique of the SPD. Any type of residual function from the Tiger montage would have to come from the text but there is nothing especially compelling about it to recommend its adoption into an oppositional vernacular, either in the manner of "everyone his own football" (as according to Walter Mehring) or in ". . . we have not only our chains to lose but our cushy posts and comfortable ministerial seats." Even the choice of an animal with some type of duplicitous characteristics would have had a little more resonance with Tarnow's (SPD's) equivocation, either by putting it in relation to other animals (animal kingdom as political body) or arising out of an immanent duplicity similar to crocodile tears. The fact that the Tiger montage was remembered in itself means less than if the memory of a photomontage is invoked within critical conjunction with a range of adversarial statements, images and sayings.

One solution within the tradition of satire (which couldn't really be applied here) is to amplify or reduce physionomic traits into the animal or vegetable kingdoms or into the land of objects. This happened to Louis Phillipe whose pin head and drooping pork-chopped jowls shouted out "pear!" long before Monnier and Daumier canonized pears to shout "Louis Phillipe!." This tactic, of course, relies upon a gratuitous bestowal by Nature and a prior public familiarity.

The dimunition of Tarnow's role in the photomontage is ex-

DAS GESICHT DES FASCHISMUS

tended by mentioning him only in his capacity as head of the Woodworkers Federation and not in his position as an SPD Reichstag Deputy. This sets up an identificatory motion carrying Tarnow personally away from actual SPD representation but returning him depersonalized as an *agent* of the "labor aristocracy" to the SPD ranks. The concept of "labor aristocracy" was used by Lenin to, among other reasons, explain why the parties of the working class of the Second International allied with their national bourgeoisies in entering WWI. It located an upper stratum of the working class who effectively controlled the parties to maintain their privilege at class expense. In the Tiger montage, this is included sub-thematically as a material basis for the SPD's hypocrisy. This was easily supported by the observable behavior of the SPD. "In the Weimar period formal clothes, banquets, state occasions, and the like became more or less routine in the lives of top party leaders. Their wives could attempt to keep up with the fashions; their sons could be sent to the university. The subjective Verbürgerlichung [bourgeoisification] of SPD leaders reached an advanced stage in our period; they did not adopt so much petty bourgeois styles of life as those of the upper orders of society."[48]

By reducing Tarnow to the role of agency, his statements are denied any individuated liberal status as opinion. The very possiblity of fleeting opinion could tag the entirety of the photomontage to a local moment and release it from its epochal standard.

Swastika Stickpin

Most elements of the photomontage fall into the purview of journalism: the Congress as event, Tarnow as "personality," the statement of SPD policy, etc. Tigers, on the other hand, being biological creatures and not historical ones, are not journalism's bill-of-fare. Neither does journalism freely recognize symbols in their raw state. The two symbols in the Tiger montage, the bourgeois clothing and the swastika stickpin, were not occasions for news. They did, however, make regular appearances in Heartfield photomontages; in fact, in his previous photomontages wherever there was a swastika a top hat was nearby. Stickpinned into the knot of the tie the swastika in the Tiger montage is not immediately disclosed.

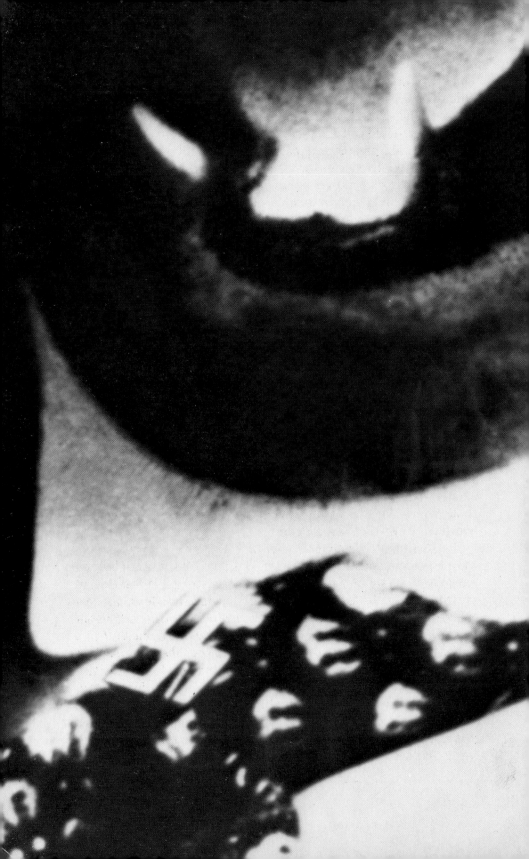

Once perceived it becomes the pivotal point around which all other elements rev- and ref-erentially revolve.

According to the Nazis, the swastika did not belong historically to Weimar. Unlike the Tiger's formal attire the swastika's runic past was pre-bourgeois and its real history could only begin when it shined down like a new day upon the 1,000-year old Reich. By 1931 the swastika, along with the Roman salute, had already achieved a full public presence. The previous year the Nazis had gained 5.5 million new votes outpolling all but the SPD. Its fevered adherents waged a pitched battle of symbology (among other battles) draping the nation with flags and banners, postering kiosks, scratching grafitti onto walls, and strutting the streets or beating on ne'er-do-wells while wearing swastika armbands. From the time of the early republic "Hackenkreuzler" (from Hackenkreuz = swastika) was used interchangably with "Nazi."

In the Tiger montage the swastika lost any autonomous reference to Naziism. Instead, it is anchored solidly into the SPD/capitalism/(Tarnow) themes. If it was to retain any autonomy with Naziism it would have had to be distanced from the tiger figure somehow. The fact that it is placed precisely is compounded by its position at the throat. This position gives it an affectivity it wouldn't have if placed, say, further down the tie or on the lapel. Malraux's maxim that one hears people's voices with the ears but one's own voice in the throat becomes amplified, so to speak, when one's voice happens to be the roar of a heavy jowled tiger choked in a tie. It is as though the wind must pass through the swastika's propellor-like structure.

The swastika's affectivity at that time was not, as it is now, so completely animated by barbarism. Besides being attached to the ideology of a naturalistic Germanicism, something the Nazis went to fantastic lengths to support, Wilhelm Reich saw the swastika's affect rooted in the response of a repressed German patriarchal sexuality to the sign's structure of "two intertwined bodies." It was a long way from the swastika's transcendance, the new day sun over the Third Reich, to two intertwined bodies. There was less psychic turf to cover in the body of the Führer, whose viscera were honored by one butcher who displayed in his window Hitler sculpted entirely in lard, parsley and sausage ends. The most kinaesthetic cohesion of community, even a community of two, was expressed by the "Heil!" and Roman salute.

During the carnival season of 1932, Ehrendorf went to a dance and picked up a tall, pretty blonde. She wore a large swastika brooch on her breast, was about nineteen or twenty, gay, uninhibited and brimful of healthy animal spirits—in short, the ideal Hitler—Mädchen. . . After the dance, Ehrendorf persuaded her to go back with him to his flat, where she met his advances more than half-way. Then at the climactic moment, the girl raised herself on one elbow, stretched out the other arm in the Roman salute, and breathed in a dying voice a fervent "Heil Hitler!" Poor Ehrendorf nearly had a stroke. When he had recovered, the blonde sweetie explained to him that she and a bunch of her girl friends had taken a solemn vow, pledging themselves "to remember the Führer every time at the most sacred moment in a woman's life." [49]

Oppositional tactics against Nazi symbology ranged from attempts to denigrate the swastika by calling it the spider or bug; to supplant it, as was attempted with the Iron Front's conscious invention of a symbol of three arrows pointing skyward along with the clenched fist greeting of "Freedom"; or to demystify it. Among the demystifcations belonged Heartfield's inclusion of "White Shame in Africa" photograph in *Deutschland, Deutschland über Alles* and the A-I-Z's 25 January 1934 article "A German Symbol?" which showed swastikas on a Buddha, Javanese puppet and a 250 ruble note from the Kerenski regime in Russia. Heartfield was able to improve on these tactics, albeit mainly after exile, by not simply emptying the sign but by reassigning a counter-significance. The most successful was "Old Motto in the 'New' Reich: Blood and Iron" (8 March 1934). The two historical throwback references are to Bismarck's 1862 slogan "Blood and Iron" for German unification through military means and the bound, bloody executioner's axes of Roman magistrate *fasces* origin, which had been proclaimed the Third Reich's official implements of execution by Göring. From *Time* magazine on 14 August 1933:

Back to the axe! Designing new costumes for himself is the delight of beefy Prussian Premier Captain Hermann Wilhelm Göring. The points of his brown shirt collar (and of his alone) are scarlet. As German Air Minister he affects a topcoat with striking white lapels. Last week he set the fashion in which Germans condemned to Death will be executed. Conqueror Napoleon introduced the French guillotine into Prussia. Last week Captain Göring banished it by decree.

White shame in Africa ▶

Fotomontage: John He[...]

Der alte Wahlspruch im „neuen" Reic[...]

BLUT UND EISEN

He substituted the medieval chopping block and headsman's axe. The headsman, he prescribed, must always wear impeccable evening dress.

Heartfield's photomontage was in response to the decapitation of four Communists. Without specific mention of them this photomontage was generalized to mean that nothing had changed since Bismarck, the stability of the nation-community was being gained only through barbarism. Its was distributed in a photographically reduced booklet into Nazi Germany. As Heartfield remembered: "Brave underground fighters from the Reich took copies over the border and so, the montages were even distributed in the big cities of the fascist barbarians. . . . My montage "Blood and Iron," showing four bloody hatchets bound together in the form of a swastika, was one of the montages which became famous because of the little A-I-Z booklet and appeared as graffiti on stone walls and was reproduced on mimeographed pamphlets."[50]

This counter-swastika was also taken up by the resistance in Germany to deface swastikas by the simple addition of curves to form the axe blades and tear-shapes for the blood. This type of transfomation differs from the origins of the swastika itself. A pre-Nazi anti-semitic organization needed a conspicuous symbol to replace the Star-of-David they obliterated from synagogue walls. Their's was a supplantation; Heartfield's four-axes was a negation. Of course, any type of defacement in Nazi Germany meant imprisonment.

Another "semioclastic" tactic was applied to the Austrian Krukenkreuz in Heartfield's photomontage "Normalization: We'll do away with this little difference," (29 July 1936) only in this instance by graphic subtraction. . . in the act of occurring!

Prior to exile Heartfield dealt with the swastika in itself only once in his 3 July 1932 "In this sign you shall be betrayed and sold" (sold down the river), a staged photomontage. In a very obvious ploy it arranges gold coins into the form of a swastika as a statement on the Nazi's connection with capital. In this way it is similar to the swastika's connection with bourgeois clothing in the Tiger montage. The swastika by itself unambiguously signifies "Naziism" and might have done the same in the Tiger montage if there had been other Nazi artifacts, events, or persons to accompany it. Without such specification it bleeds off into the other com-

91

Normalisierung

Der deutschen Kolonie in Österreich soll eine angemessene Mög-
lichkeit zur gesellschaftlichen Betätigung gegeben werden.

Aus dem Abkommen zwischen Deutschland und Österreich über die Normalisierung der Beziehungen.

Dieses Zeichen

österreichische

Diese kleine Differenz werden wir auch noch aus der Welt schaffe

ponents of the photomontage, something seemingly absurd. Although the SPD may have tolerated the "constitutional dictator-ship" of Brüning they certainly had no truck with the Nazis. Yet the Hackenkreuz and SPD are not differentiated in the photomontage. They are, in fact, equated under "fascism." The Nazis did not call themselves "fascists," only a wing of Stahlhelm (Steel Helmets), the independent army of nationalists, did so. Not coming from any self-definition within Weimar, "fascism" instead came from Stalin and the Comintern, the German Communist Party and, of course, Heartfield.

Social Fascism

The concept of social democratic fascism was tied up in the "third period" of communist strategic phases. The first period began with the Russian Revolution's triggering of international revolutionary mobilization and ended with the capitalist stability of 1924. 1928 was the beginning of the "third period;" it signaled an end of stabil-ity, the beginning of deep capitalist crisis and a "new phase of revolutionary upsurge," which could potentially inaugurate the epoch of socialism in Germany. These were the findings of the Sixth Congress of the Comintern in 1928, a year when the capital-ist nations still enjoyed stability and nothing could be construed as a revolutionary trend among the working classes. The Sixth Con-gress analysis was meant to characterize the moment; when it turned out to foretell the crisis, its pre-science lent a confidence in the truth value of its theoreticisms at the sufferance of observable phenomena.

In Germany, the inability to determine what constituted a revo-lutionary uprising—e.g., economist strikes, confrontations with police—was indicative of the KPD's purely oppositional status. Its power was chimeric when it came to what the working class was and wasn't ready to undertake. Although the KPD may have had a higher percentage of working class as members the higher percent-age of the working class were members of the SPD. From 1924 until Brüning the KPD's Reichstag voting was not substantially dif-ferent from the SPD and after Brüning voting didn't much matter. In contrast to the SPD what the KPD had effectively rallied was the specter of conscience. According to Wilhelm Reich, "Everyone knew that the Communists were correct in principle, from a Marxist-scientific standpoint. But on practical everyday issues, the Social Democrats seemed to be in the right."[51]

The Social Democrats were in a position to be "correct" on practical everyday issues of the working class, being at the time equated with issues of conscription into capitalist industry, because they controlled the labor unions. This control, of course, was the throne of their heresy.

The association of social democracy with fascism was formulated by Stalin not long before the Sixth Congress: "Fascism is the bourgeoisie's fighting organization that relies on the active support of Social Democracy. Social Democracy is objectively the *moderate* wing of Fascism. These organizations do not negate but supplement each other. They are not antipodes, they are twins. Fascism is an informal political bloc of these two chief organizations."

The "informality" of this political bloc had to do with the proximity of both to capital. The failure of this formulation was to perceive capital as monolithic and not to account for the specific factions of capital with which the social democrats and "fascists" were in alliance. Nevertheless, any distinction that had existed between social democracy and fascism vanished when the 10th Plenum of the Comintern (July 1929) eliminated the "moderation" while introducing "Social Fascism" into the prescribed communist vocabulary: "The aims of the Fascists and Social Fascists are the same; the difference consists in the slogans and partly also in the methods. There is also a certain difference in that 'pure' Fascism does not employ any left wing, while to Social Fascism such a wing is absolutely necessary. It is the special task of the left wing of Social Fascism to operate with pacifist, democratic and 'socialist' slogans."

By Fall 1929 the term had become embedded in the daily vocabulary of the KPD. Even before the Müller cabinet had ceded to Brüning, Ernst Thälmann, chairman of the KPD from 1925, remarked that "the rule of fascism has already been established in Germany." When the SPD tolerated Brüning's Center Party it only supplied Thälmann with further evidence. "In pursuing its fascist course the present policy of the German bourgeoisie is characterized by its unique alternating use of the SPD and Hitler's Party, with the SPD still functioning as the principal social prop for the bourgeoisie."

He called attempts to question such sweeping characterizations "steps-theories" by people "indulging in minute calculations of percentages and degrees of German fascism."

The threat of Nazi rule was diminished by the KPD because the "Nazi fools would make lousy bureaucrats," and, in any case, the party which shared the bourgeoisie with the SPD would naturally succumb to the bourgeois crisis which had worked its wonders on the SPD. In probably the most absurd and disastrous of communist scenarios for late-Weimar, the Nazis were to aid in the eradication of the SPD. The "fascistization" of the SPD which would lead to a Nazi takeover would alienate the working class from the SPD and, once the Nazis failed, the workers would "awaken" and embrace a KPD bereft of competition from either authoritarians or heretics.

All this was the substance of a group discussion in Wieland Herzfelde's apartment that the Austrian Ernst Fischer (at that time a journalist, later known for his popularization of Marx and writings on art) chronicled:

—Hitler in power?
—Won't ever happen!
—Let him come! In a year's time he'd be played out, if not before. Then it'll be our turn!

This exchange took place in the flat of the Communist publisher Wieland Herzfelde. The room was full of people sitting about on chairs, tables, boxes. One little man was perched up on a cupboard. This was John Heartfield, the brilliant inventor of photomontage.

—(Ernst Fischer) Once Hitler's in power he'll be there to stay.
—Now listen! Do you know what the German proletariat's like?
—(EF) I know what Italian Fascism's like. Mussolini. . .
—Germany isn't Italy. The battle-hardened KPD. . .
—He's never come across 'em. He's from Vienna.
—Of course. The Austro-Marxist variant.
—Hitler's a puppet of monopoly capitalism and, though he doesn't know it and his backers don't see it, he's a blind tool of history. He's paving the way. . .
—(EF) Who for?
—For us, of course. The class instinct of many proletarians has not yet reached the stage of revolutionary class consciousness. For them, Social Democracy's finished, but they're not yet rallying to

us. They vote for Hitler. His function consists in detaching them from Social Democracy. Then, when he disappoints their hopes, they'll come over to us. It's self-evident.

—(EF) Is it as self-evident as all that?

There was a regular set-to between Communists. Soon everyone was talking at once. Wieland Herzfelde tried to keep some semblance of order. "Let him finish what he's saying!" Interjections, complete bedlam. "Give him a chance to speak!" I remained silent, listening. So there was some hope here afterall, a clash of opinions, a search for a new concept, an orientation toward a united front. Suddenly a voice cut through the din. It came from the top of the cupboard where John Heartfield was sitting.

—(JH) Comrades! I demand that this discussion cease instantly! There's a Social Fascist in our midst!

I looked about me. Silence. Who could it be?

—(JH) It's completely inadmissable to discuss internal party matters in the presence of a Social Fascist!

I turned my head this way and that. Silence. Everyone was looking at me. So I was the Social Fascist. I rose to my feet in embarassment and took my leave.[52]

Several conditions existed, some genuine others inglorious, which led perfectly intelligent people to become leaflet-brained on the matter of social fascism. One was the consistent track record of the SPD's antagonism toward the KPD, beginning with Gustav Noske and the assassinations of Liebknecht and Luxemburg and highlighted in late-Weimar by the murders of communist demonstrators under the direction of Zörgiebel. As mentioned the last photomontage of 1931, "Fraternal Greetings from the SPD" showed the corpse of Liebknecht to jolt memory into indignation. Rosa Luxemburg was not shown in the photomontage. Her body was retrieved after weeks in the river so the corpse was not stately—although photographs existed. Some other type of commemoration could have been constructed within Heartfield's photomontage. But in late-Weimar Rosa Luxemborg was falling from Stalinist grace. Her assassination had dealt a serious blow to an autonomous theoretical practice by German communists, one stressing German specificities; her censure guaranteed that the standard she had set would not be acknowledged. The standard acknowledged instead was that of the simple-minded Thälmann who was fully sanctioned, at times recuperated, by Stalin who, of all the once contending successors to Lenin, knew least of European realities.

> It is said that theoretical knowledge is not a strong point with the present [KPD] Central Committee. . . The strength of the Central Committee lies in the fact that it pursues a correct Leninist policy, and that is something which the puny intellectuals who pride themselves on their "knowledge" refuse to recognize. . . Comrade Thälmann, use the services of these intellectuals if they really want to serve the cause of the working class, or send them to the devil if they are determined to command at all costs.

These sentiments followed the party line down through the ranks, squelching what inner-party debate remained. Dissent always carried threat of expulsion. For the many whose employment was with the party this meant being further disciplined by Germany's tremendous unemployment (in the early-30s, one in three was fully employed). The most trenchant critique of the German situation came from Trotsky, who had already been expelled and whose position as object of constant derision no right-minded German Communist would contemplate imitating. His counterpart Stalin was back in Russia practicing his position as the exhortative object in patrimony of Lenin ("Snow White" as Oskar Maria Graf called Lenin in his glass coffin), of which some leaked down to Thälmann.

However, probably the most compelling contributing factor was the condition of post-revolutionary Russia; for many this was the pudding to prove any point. Arthur Koestler, famed for his renunciative tossing the Marxist baby out with the Soviet bath water, felt required in "The Promethean Vision" to make the following observation:

> Every comparison between the state of affairs in Russia and the Western world seemed to speak eloquently in favor of the former. In the West, there was mass unemployment; in Russia a shortage of manpower. In the West, chronic strikes and social unrest which, in some countries, were threatening to lead to civil war; in Russia, where all factories belonged to the people, the workers vied in socialist competitions for higher production outputs. In the West, the anarchy of laissez-faire was drowning the capitalist system in chaos and depression; in Russia, the First Five Year Plan was transforming, by a series of giant strokes, the most backward into the

most advanced country in Europe. If History herself were a fellow-traveller, she could not have arranged a more clever timing of events than this coincidence of the gravest crisis of the Western world with the initial phase of Russia's industrial revolution. The contrast between the downward trend of capitalism and the simultaneous steep rise of planned Soviet economy was so striking and obvious that it led to the equally obvious conclusion: they are the future—we, the past.

The sense of representing the future had been part of the avant-gardist temperament Heartfield came out of as well as the orthodox Marxism in which he was tutored. This utopic component had always had to play itself out temporally; with the development of Russia, however, it was spatial, concurrent and at all odds with the anarchronistic death fidgets of Weimar. Seemingly, with such a living model to the east there would be little action required to put the degenerate Weimarian dinosaur out of its misery. Yet there was inactivity and stasis.

On her visit to Berlin Simone Weil had the "impression that the German workers are not at all disposed to capitulate, but they are incapable of fighting."[53] In a number of respects, Kracauer's description of Neue Sachlichkeit had become socialized: "Neue Sachlichkeit marks a state of paralysis. Cynicism, resignation, disillusionment: these tendencies point to a mentality disinclined to commit itself in any direction. . . The main feature of the new realism is its reluctance to ask questions, to take sides."[54]

The main difference from the "relative stability" which gave rise to Neue Sachlichkeit and the highly politicized atmosphere of the late-Weimar instability, was that in the early-30s it did not ultimately matter if one possessed a "mentality disinclined to commit itself" since no commitment could prove satisfactory. Open channels of action were lacking.

The Socialist and Communist fatalism demobilized, respectively, by constant postponement of ruling class dismantlement or by relying on the march of history to shape events (since the KPD was not in a position of political power to do so). There was also a profound inertia attendant upon the Communists' pedagogical and propagandistic concepts. At its basis was the superstition that "truth makes its own way in the world," as Ernst Bloch wrote. To pique class consciousness all that was necessary was to point to the historical signposts or, rather, to the Enlightenment lamp posts so the workers will "awaken." Bloch's observation that "the Nazis speak falsely, but to people, the communists truthfully, but of things," is demonstrated in a rally described by Wilhelm Reich.

> I remember one enormous meeting in a sports stadium where Thälmann addressed about twenty thousand industrial and white-collar workers. Shortly before, there had been fatalities at a demonstration. The atmosphere was highly charged. The opening by the flag bearers was impressive. Tensely, we waited for the address. Thälmann deflated our high spirits within half an hour; he nullified them by outlining the complicated budget of the German bourgeoisie. It was horrible. The effect of this pseudo-scientific "education to class-consciousness" with the aid of high-flown politics was particularly catastrophic in the youth organizations.

In addition to an inherent incompatability of vanguardism and pedagogy, the KPD's lack of a politics of subjectivity came disastrously to the fore as late-Weimar was politicized (activity within the realm of culture was no guarantee for subjectivity). This realm was abdicated to the Nazis whose contradictory ideologies grafted themselves gelatinously onto the equivocations of the period.

Of any of the reasons, the most paralytic was the inability for the two parties of the working class, the SPD and KPD, to form any type of alliance against Naziism and the ascendant Right. At different times, leading up to Hitler's assumption of power 30 January 1933 and for a short period thereafter, electoral or parliamentary alliances, even of a temporary character, or coordination of general strikes or armed uprisings by the SPD and KPD could have prevented the Nazis from coming into rule.

In response to their party's inactivity some SPD activists formed the Iron Front in January 1931 to organize opposition to Naziism. Some left the party altogether and joined with independents to form the Socialist Workers Party. In common with a number of "left-wing intellectuals" these groups called for working class unity. They were vociferous and made their positions known. However, their numbers were relatively small, their influence negligible in the face of the larger parties' intransigence, and many of their signals were contradictory.

The KPD throughout late-Weimar promoted a "united front" to the activist rank-and-file of the working class. But it was a so-called "united front from below" whose ultimate motive was a draining off of SPD rank-and-file and a swelling of KPD ranks. The cynicism of this maneuver, which did not go unnoticed, is repeated in Heartfield's 24 June 1932 poster "Red Unity will set you free!" Three bicep-laden male factory worker arms hold the shaft of a red flag. The top arm bears the hammer and sickle, next the three arrows of the Iron Front, third the bare arm of the unaffiliated. More important than the hierarchical arrangement of these symbols is the fact that the poster was a KPD election poster encouraging the viewer to "Vote List 3", i.e., the KPD slate. It was also part of the KPD-initiated "Anti-Fascist Action" of May 1932, which mobilized thousands but was too little too late and had no chance of succeeding without official SPD participation on some level.

In general, stasis was imposed upon the workers by the actions of the two main parties. Although the labor unions were divided along partisan lines there were cultural and sports organizations where the working class formed a social united front, if not a political one, outside party proscriptions. Reich spoke of a similar impulse at a December 1932 demonstration in the Lustgarten.

> Communist organizations, in particular the Kampfbünde (Fighting Unions), joined the demonstration. They mingled with the mass of the Social Democratic demonstrators, and without any talk about U.S./Japanese contradictions, they formed a united front. That was the will and language of the masses. The KPD leaders, who wanted a united front "only under Communist leadership," later reprimanded the party members concerned. The party orders had only been to line the streets and to "cheer" the demonstration.

Around the same time members of SPD organizations, the Reichsbanner and Iron Front, were itching for armed attacks against the Nazis but the party never gave the go ahead signal. Once the Nazis had taken over they were instructed to "lie still".

The KPD, on the other hand, went through preparations anticipating (Bolshevist) illegality but never committed itself to preventing illegality from occurring. They explained away the Nazis' 14 September 1930 electoral success as their zenith, from which point it would be all downhill. This hill, of course, turned out to be Sisyphian. On the front cover of the 1 January 1933 issue of A-I-Z a Heartfield photomontage shows Hitler, a capitalist and his top hat,

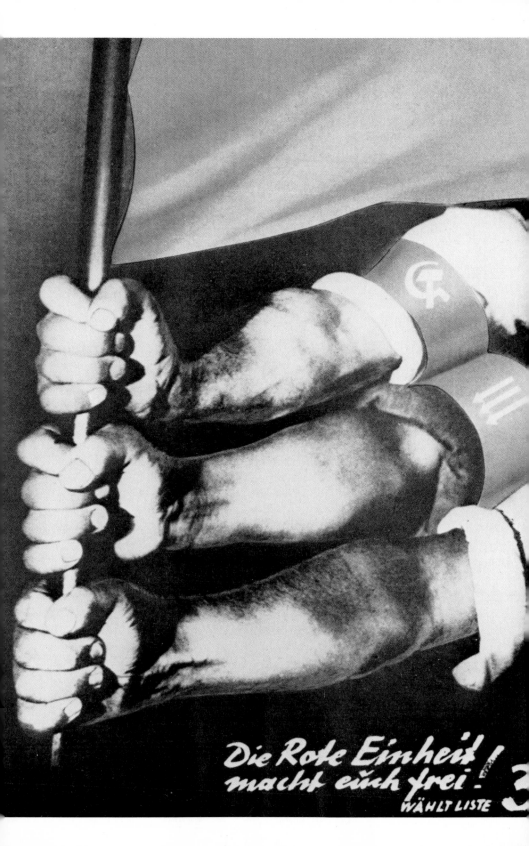

Die Rote Einheit!
macht euch frei!
WÄHLT LISTE 3

and a crumbling swastika tumbling down a rocky edifice— "A-I-Z wishes a bon voyage in the new year!" Hitler became chancellor at the end of the month. Two months later, after the Nazi repression and the KPD flight to Prague following the Reichstag fire, the Executive Committee of the Comintern issued a resolution which included:

> The present quiet after the victory of fascism is no more than a passing phase. In spite of the fascist terror, Germany's revolutionary upsurge will continue inexorably. . . The establishment of open fascist dictatorship, which destroys all the democratic illusions of the masses and frees them from the influence of Social Democracy, speeds up the process of Germany's evolution towards proletarian revolution.

The pathos continued until the time of the Popular Front when the cooperation between the two parties didn't matter anymore because a potentially effective mass base of resistance in Germany had since been lost.

Epochalyptic

Two consequences of the adoption of the doctrine of social fascism—a worsening of the likelihood to form a bloc against Naziism and the dimunition of the perceived threat of Naziism—were contributed to by the Tiger montage. Nothing was explicitly done in the photomontage to allow an SPD rank-and-file escape from the accusations upon the party's leadership. This would have been preferable, of course, only if severence of SPD members from the ranks could be justified over collaboration, no matter how fleeting, against the Nazis. In the photomontage a full presence of the Nazis was drained from the swastika reducing their socio-political existence to a sign generating role, one below that of the SPD which had usurped the lion's share of all the "fascism" to be had in the swastika. For the KPD member, by generalizing any object of attack into "fascism" the photomontage fails to narrow a course of action, not that meeting times had to be listed; all specificity was only to be found orbiting out of reach in the ozone of the epoch where courses of action take on a (science) fictive form. The photomontage gave the appearance that this elevation was a reading of historical materialism *out of* events, ensuring a requisite accuracy before manifesting itself in all the exagerations and hyperbole granted art. But it was a reading *onto* events, an historicizing in reverse, the imposition of epoch and agency.

Since the KPD wasn't in a position to determine the direction of the republic, the majority of the working class being allegiant to the SPD (esp. being the ones with jobs and the capacity to strike), they could rationalize a further deterioration in the crisis of capital because it promised, in their ideology of crisis and revolution, a precipitation of the proletariat into their ranks. That is, since the KPD could not possess political control of the German working class in the present it possessed the inevitability of their consciousness, the afterlife of their political being. The degree to which Heartfield internalized this lent unfortunate accuracy to being characterized as "the purest of all communist intellectuals in Germany" by his Russian monographer Sergei Tretyakov.

The unfortunate irony is that by rising above events and conditions the Tiger montage parallels the transcendant aesthetics which achieve their distance no less insidiously and run the same risk of being scuttled by what they avoid.

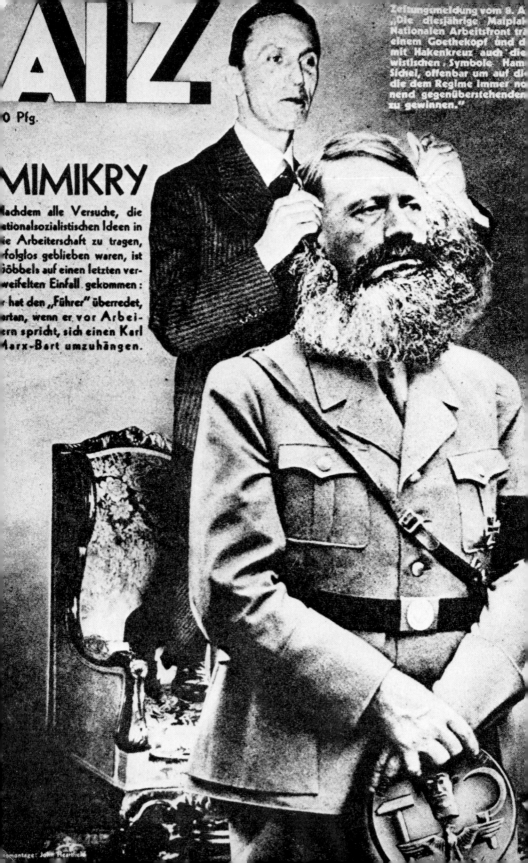

AIZ

0 Pfg.

Zeitungsmeldung vom 8. A
„Die diesjährige Maiplak
Nationalen Arbeitsfront trä
einem Goethekopf und d
mit Hakenkreuz auch die
wistischen Symbole Ham
Sichel, offenbar um auf di
die dem Regime immer no
nend gegenüberstehenden
zu gewinnen."

MIMIKRY

Nachdem alle Versuche, die
nationalsozialistischen Ideen in
die Arbeiterschaft zu tragen,
erfolglos geblieben waren, ist
Göbbels auf einen letzten ver-
zweifelten Einfall gekommen:
er hat den „Führer" überredet,
ertan, wenn er vor Arbei-
tern spricht, sich einen Karl
Marx-Bart umzuhängen.

Photomontage: John Heartfield

MONTAGE, MIMIKRY

This section situates Heartfield's work by comparing it to an array of practices. First, it is set against an expanded notion of montage based on the principles of combination; then against the genre of compilation films. This genre, which took place in the 20s and 30s in Europe and Russia, is not well known in the U.S. yet it proves to be a much better cinematic comparison than the usual comparisons with the film montage of Sergei Eisenstein. Like Heartfield's work, compilation films used pre-existing cultural material—photojournalism and other films, respectively—thus, this comparison provides a narrowed and more accurate location within montage. A newly formulated cultural category of "mimikry" is presented through its actions to illuminate this specificity within montage. Mimikry is then used as a vantage point to observe recent cultural actions; this is a preferable lineage to emphasize because as a model for opposition it offers greater mobility among media and disciplines, official and unofficial cultural sites, than would tracing the direct influence of Heartfield within photomontage. This section ends with speculation on actual simulation as an extension of a repressive use of mimikry.

Montage

Artistic montage officially raised its scattered head in Berlin. Heartfield went public with the word April 1920 in *dada 3* as Monteurdada (from a Francophiled Mr. Montage-monsieur) and "John Heartfield, mont.", the signature on the cover collage. This was after the photomontage on the cover of *Jedermann. . .* and long before "montage" and "photo" would be connected in consistent practice. The Berlin Dadaists cited 1916 as the date of the "invention" of photomontage. This claim was made in retrospect by both Grosz and Heartfield on the one side and Raoul Hausmann and Hannah Höch on the other. Any claim, however, could be rightfully made only to the introduction of photomontage into avantgarde art—"In fact," as Herzfelde put it, "photomontage was more discovery than invention."—for the simple fact that the second half of the 19th century is full of examples of photomontage. There were those photographers such as O.G. Rejlander and Henry Peach Robinson who used photomontage to fuel academic art; idiosynchratic examples such as the theosophistic, multiple döppelganger photography of the remarkable inhabitant of Vancouver Island, Hannah Maynard; montage used as a technique to circumvent various technological limitations; the popular photography such as the postcards of impossible imagery (jackalopes and boat-sized trout) that is still with us; etc. There were plenty in circulation before the 20th century, before the cubism which was supposed to have engendered montage, and before WWI when the (proto) dadaists discovered it.

If photomontage's formal ancestry was not made evident to Heartfield soon after his claims to invention were made, he would have been thoroughly convinced after seeing the reproductions in a 1931 issue of *Die Arbeite Fotograf* of Eugene Appert's right-wing photomontage reconstructions of and immediately following the Paris Commune. In any case, artistic authorship was not on Heartfield's agenda so much as artistic development. Hausmann, on the other hand, clung to authorship to his French deathbed in 1971, fending off Grosz/Heartfield, Max Ernst, the Russian Gustav Klutsis, even dropping Hannah Höch who was with him at the time of his "invention." From his book *Courrier Dada*:

It was on the occasion of a visit to the Baltic seacoast on the island of Usedom in the little village of Heidebrink, that I conceived the idea of photomontage. On the walls of almost every house was a colored lithograph depicting the image of a grenadier against a background of barracks. To make this military memento more personal, a photographic portrait of a soldier had been used in place of the head. This was like a stroke of lightning, one could—I saw it instantly—make paintings entirely composed of cut-out photographs.

Hausmann's passive appropriation (from folk art) into an elevated realm (fine art, "anti" or not) should be compared to the antimilitarist dissent within the vulgar realm of WWI which delineates Grosz and Heartfield's first use.

With its early-20s incidence in Germany and Russia, "montage" carried the class connotations on either side of "construction": the working class which does the construction and the intelligentsia which conceives of the construction—engineers, scientists and artists. There were also the mechanotopic connotations which pervaded vanguard and avant-garde alike. However, no matter how much talk surrounded photomontage, heroic images of mechanization found relatively little place in the images, possibly because sufficient valorization existed by the fact a machine was in on every image to begin with.

Within the post-war Berlin artistic circles, Monteuranzüge (overalls) could be worn to express proletarian partisanship while countering the flowing garb of the more flamboyant Expressionists. Hausmann wrote that the adoption of "monteur" was based in "our refusal to play the part of the artist. We regarded ourselves as engineers and our work as construction: we assembled (Fr. - monter) our work, like a fitter." In contrast to artists thinking of themselves as engineers, the Russian Revolution interrupted Eisenstein's training as an actual engineer, propelling him into theater and eventually to film. From a philosophical unity he found in dialectical materialism he sought a departure point at an intersection of science/technology and art. Speaking of himself in the third person:

Don't forget it was a young engineer who was bent on finding a scientific approach to the secrets and mysteries of art. The disciplines he had studied had taught him one thing: in every scientific investigation there must be a unit of measurement. So he set out in search of the unit of impression produced in art! Science knows *ions*, *electrons*, and *neutrons*. Let there be *attraction* in art. Everyday language borrowed from industry a word denoting the assembling of machinery, pipes, machine tools. This striking word is *montage* which means assembling, and though it is not yet in vogue, it has every qualification to become fashionable.[55]

Eisenstein was the one who most energetically theorized the concept of montage. He did this after montage was established in Germany. Mayakovsky had visited Berlin in 1922 taking Grosz, Heartfield and Hausmann photomontages back to the circles of the Russian journal LEF. Hausmann reported that El Lissitsky visited his studio the same year. The 1923 article "Montage of Attractions", Eisenstein's first writing on the subject, cited "Grosz's *storehouse of images* and Rodchenko's *elements of photo-illustration*" as sources for montage—not for film, however, for theater.

After Berlin Dada, Hausmann effectively quit making photo-montages, Höch being the only one besides Heartfield to contin-ue. The early dadaist innovations and developments soon found their way, primarily through the Bauhaus commercialist conduit, into the Weimar advertising industry. Apart from being superior to most, Heartfield's bookcovers were in no way contrary to advertis-ing. By the late-20s with mass reproductive technology and in-stitutions fully in place photomontage was widespread. The Nazis and Italian Fascists also had their photomontages, ranging in scale from magazines to billboards.

Of the Germans, Heartfield was synonymous with montage, whereas the term assumed lesser value for other practitioners. Within left modernism, especially literature and theater, montage became intertwined with documentary and reportage. It was associated with methods and formal organizations of material and as an essential element in juxtaposing "appearance and reality." An ascendant social realism moved toward discouraging montage up to the fully formulated attacks at the 1934 Soviet Writers' Con-gress (where, by the way, Herzfelde argued for the modernism of the writers he had published). As the vise tightened around the modernist left, Lukacs, the theoretical adjudicator of communist anti-modernism, granted Heartfield reprieve while pronouncing sentence on authors and dramatists.

In montage's original form as photomontage, it is capable of striking effects and on occasion it can even become a powerful political weapon. Such effects arise from its technique of juxtaposing heterogeneous, unrelated pieces of reality torn from their context. A good photomontage has the same effect as a good joke. [56]

Any attempt, however, to go past this "one-dimensional technique—however successful it may be in a joke," to extend past the momentary tasks of photomontage into more encompassing narrative forms, only results in "profound monotony." As it turned out monotony was grounds for punishment.

The other strain of modernism relating to montage is that beginning with the works of "Baudelaire, Courbet, Rimbaud and Lautrèamont" in the 19th century. André Breton, in a May 1935 interview, distinguished this strain of "non-conformist" art from work with "immediately polemical social characteristics, such as the work of Daumier."[57] In the 20th century, the art of Grosz, Dix, Kollwitz, et. al. (coincidentally all German), should not be seen as the only inherently political form; in fact, it is a secondary genre, a subset of the products of an artistic imagination which "stands aside from any fidelity to circumstance, especially the *intoxicating* circumstances of history."

From this current of modernism came a tactilism, a *material* handling of language and a materiality of signification in general. Attendant upon this was the reduction of things to a de-differentiated surface where the entire world of reference was liberated, open to poetic purview and accessible. Simple juxtaposition could dislodge anything caught in a web of received relationships and precipitate it by attachment to a new relationship. Lautrèamont valorized as much in his paean of beauty, "The chance encounter, on a dissecting table, of a sewing machine and an umbrella." Reverdy brought it to greater conscious disposal in his idea of the image: "The more the relation between the two realities is distant and accurate, the stronger the image will be— the more it will possess emotional power and poetic reality." According to Hausmann, Johannes Baader and he celebrated the centennial of Gottfried Keller in an impromptu manner by standing in the middle of a street reading from here and there in Keller's *Der grüne Heinrich*, creating "marvelous combinations". Raymond Roussel used overt procedures in constructing his novel *Im-*

pressions of Africa. And Tristan Tzara worked literally with processes of materiality in his cut-up poems which were read in randomly selected fragments.

Much earlier, Edgar Allan Poe described how his protagonist in the "Literary Life of Thingum Bob, Esq.," through a simple physical technique, became the leading lacerating critic Thomas Hawk.

> My practice was this. I bought auction copies (cheap) of "Lord Brougham's Speeches," "Cobbett's Complete Works," the "New Slang-Syllabus," the "Whole Art of Snubbing," "Prentice's Billingsgate" (folio edition), and "Lewis G. Clarke on Tongue." These works I cut up thoroughly with a curry-comb and then, throwing the shreds into a sieve, sifted out carefully all that might be thought decent (a mere trifle); reserving the hard phrases, which I threw into a large tin pepper-castor with longitudinal holes, so that an entire sentence could get through without material injury. . . . I anointed a sheet of foolscap with the white of a gander's egg; then, shredding the thing to be reviewed as I had previously shredded the books— only with more care so as to get to every word separate—I threw the latter shreds in with the former, screwed on the lid of the castor, gave it a shake, and so dusted out the mixture upon the egged foolscap, where it stuck.

The reviews (hatchet jobs) he produced with this method were quite successful, except when certain fragments and sentences remained upside down. But fragments from "Mr. Lewis Clark's paragraphs. . . were so vigorous and altogether stout, that they seemed not particularly disconcerted by any extreme of position, but looked equally happy and satisfactory whether on their heads or on their heels."

Much earlier still, medieval Hebrew poets in Spain not only "took" themes from the Old Testament, they went one step further by cutting out phrases and sentences, combining and integrating them into their own writings. Here, literature of revelation and redemption was worked upon as an object, as material directed into an auto-genesis: in the reworking, the Bible would still be spoken. This "mosaic style" belonged to the linguistic mysticism of the 13th century Kabbalists. One of the most important, Abraham Abulafia, developed a method of combining letters which, by being singularly inert in the world but charged with the unspoken name of God, brought the meditator into ecstatic commune with

God. After some preparation ". . . take ink, pen and a table to thy hand and remember that thou art about to serve God in joy of the gladness of heart. Now begin to combine a few or many letters, to permute and to combine them until thy heart be warm. Then be mindful of their movements and of what thou canst bring forth by moving them. And when thou feelst that thy heart is already warm and when thou seest that by combination of letters thou canst grasp new things which by human tradition or by thouself thou wouldst not be able to know and when thou art thus prepared to receive the influx of divine power which flows into thee." A meditation upon the resultant configuration brings about a strong "intellectual influx" which weakens "thy outer and thy inner parts" such that "thy whole body will be seized by an extremely strong trembling."[58]

Instead of divine power flowing into thee, as with Abulafia's solo soliloquy to God, Heartfield had another goal for his meditations, a Pavlovian agit-prop effect flowing out of thee. In a speech in Moscow in 1931 he said, "If I gather documents, arrange them and do this skillfully then the agitational-propagandistic effect upon the masses will be powerful." Instead of a "lonely house where none shall hear thy voice . . . prayer shawl and tefillin . . . cleanse thy clothes and, if possible, let all they garmets be white. . .", Heartfield "burrows in the photo libraries for hours, for days, looking for a suitable photo of Hermann Müller, Hugenburg, Röhm, whoever is needed." he had built his own photo archives of sorts (or, rather, of unsorts)—"Clippings from newspapers and archives of sorts lay on top of and under his work table." However, both created and worked through their immersions, a concentrative abandon amid a greatly expanded field, by combinatory practices: Abulafia with letters and Heartfield (in a German language noted for endless combinatory word formation) with significations.

The type of opening for Abulafia where "thou canst grasp new things which by human tradition or by thyself thou wouldst not be able to know . . ." also could work for Heartfield and can in any combinatory practice. New possibilities, the unexpected, accidental, the *intoxicating* apart from and in conjunction with the "intoxicating circumstances of history" are predisposed by the method. More so than in other artistic processes because the material itself contributes. Matters could possibly come down to the removal of a few impediments.

Heartfield did not unleash this process to the fullest extent, yet even in a very proscribed problem in a commissioned work the fragment which initially suggests or finally coheres the photomontage may not have been encountered otherwise; it would have been, therefore, "heaven sent." In immersion, by placing oneself in a dialogical position to a large (certainly greater than an individual's memory or recall—since these are the very things piqued), yet consistent body of material where, through transient combination and fixed trial combinations, the material takes over some of the production, the producer consumes from the very beginning. With possibilities suggested by the encounter with a massive body of particularized information, stretching to the extraneous and back and, through combination, adding to this mass what was not there to begin with, the producer can function more cogently as a pre-emptive receiver, a proto-consumer with this sneak preview structured into the production process.

One basic distinction between combinatory practices is found in the general disposition toward the material. If the material is sacred, the disposition devotional and the material of a domain whose power is seen as desirable in extending, it will be quite different from Heartfield who worked critically with the vulgar to destroy it. He could only be repulsed. Not only was he a "determined hater of photographers" but their products, his raw material, represented the personalities, class and system to which he was intransigently opposed. Any redemption had to be conceived arising from an historical supercession of both his material and his role; he sought the obsolesence of both. Heartfield was not the devotee butcher who created a portrait of Hitler out of lard, parsley and sausage ends. He was on the other alimentary end altogether, the type of media worker Enzensberger had in mind when he noted that "the fear of handling shit is a luxury a sewerman cannot necessarily afford."

One of the recompenses Heartfield could point to was his role in facilitating adversaries to speak for themselves authenticating their own indictment through confession. If anything, this would expedite the material's destruction. The material speaking for itself relieved Heartfield from any public appearance, where his presence/authorship could distract. This is puppetry with real people, ventriloquism with actual voices, a parody performed by the object of parody, not the object speaking through the parodist as in imitation. Within the practice of montage contemporary with Heartfield, this characteristic was shared by the genre of compilation films.

Compilation Films

Film has montage in its very innards. The projector runs just fast enough so images cannot be seen as they butt up against each other and just slow enough so the images are not superimposed. The former would be photography, the latter photomontage, a narrativity of film squeezed into a form not conducive to it.

The mere contiguity of the frames constitutes a technical montage by way of juxtaposition and differentiation, no matter if no difference in adjacent images exists. Formal montage is in the cutting of the film, cutting to different scenes; it goes with the technical turf. In sharing photography and montage, comparisons between film and photomontage are sensible, just as they are common amid photomontage talk. But the technical and formal aspects of film have overwhelmed a lone, under-theorized photomontage resulting in unsatisfactory comparisons in the realm of practice.

In the chapter on montage in *From Caligari to Hitler* Kracauer discusses the "cross-cut" films of the Weimar Republic. The films are exemplified by *Berlin: A Symphony of a Great City* which took a cinematic sampling, a "splice of life" of the city and set it to a presentation denoting rhythm and music. The genre as a whole was strangely void of sociality, a depopulation owing to Neue Sachlichkeit. And, as Tucholsky might have said about them, they were "official cross sections" since they "always cut the cheese without hitting the maggots." As such, they had no compelling similarity to Heartfield's work.

Comparisons to Eisenstein's film are made probably because he theorized montage and Heartfield did not, a fact toward which present day preoccupations with theory would naturally gravitate. It relates inadequately to Heartfield's work since the material Eisenstein edited was original whereas Heartfield's work largely depended upon the familiarity garnered from pre-shot shots.

A more accurate comparison can be found in the films of Esfir Shub, the Russian filmmaker. She taught Eisenstein how to edit; actually, she taught him re-editing. They worked on the Fritz Lang film *Dr. Mabuse*, rearranging it to become Shub's *Gilded Putrefication*. In her 1927 film, *Fall of the Romanov Dynasty*, she utilized several thousand feet of the Tsar's home movies in combination with old newsreels. The rummaging she did resembled the rummaging of Heartfield: "The *Fall of the Romanov Dynasty* and my following two films filled three years with the joy of searching, finding, "opening" historical film-documents—but not in film libraries or archives, for there were no such things then. In the damp cellars of Goskino, in "Kino Moskva", in the Museum of the Revolution lay boxes of negatives and random prints, and no one knew how they had got there."[59]

The making of such films out of old and foreign films was originally necessitated by the scarcity of raw footage. Kuleshov's *On the Red Front* was such an example during the shortages of the civil war. Even the critic Viktor Shklovsky participated, "We re-montaged the American films we received in minor ways but skillfully and cheerfully."

Compilation films were made outside Russia as well. The Dutch filmmaker Joris Ivens describes his "idea editing" in *The Camera and I*.

> My earliest experience was some time in 1929 when I was given charge of the film programs for a series of workers' cultural and educational Sunday mornings. On Friday nights we would borrow a number of commercial newsreels. On Saturday we would study the material in the newsreels in relation to the international and national situation of the week, re-edit them with any other footage we happened to have available to us giving them a clear political significance, print new subtitles (the films were still silent) showing relationships between events which newsreel companies never thought of, and which would certainly have shocked them if they had ever seen our uses of their "innocent" material. For example, we could relate the injustice of an American lynching with the injustice of the Japanese aggression in Manchuria, making a general statement about injustice which we would then localize with a current event in our own country. Previously miscellaneous material was knit together into a new unity, sometimes with the addition of a spoken word on the public address system or some cartoons, photographs

JAHRGANG VIII 1929
NR. 25
20 Pf.
15 Kon.
40 Gr.
30 Cent.

BISHER
NN
EN
R

SCHEINT AB NR. 27 ZWANZIGSE

A-I-Z

IE ARBEITER ZEITUNG ALLER LÄNDER

PUDOWKI
der berühmte Regisseur von „St
über Asien" und der „Letzten T
von St. Petersburg" prüft die F
streifen des neuen deutsch-russisc
Gemeinschaftsfilms der Meschrabp
Prometheus

„Das Leben ist schö

or photostats or a editorial from the Dutch conservative press. After cur Sunday morning show was finished we would take the film apart again, restore its original form and return it to the newsreel companies who were none the wiser!

The best known compilation film was screened only once, in 1928 by the Popular Association for Film Art in Berlin. Sponsors of the Association represented a relatively broad political spectrum for the left, including Heinrich Mann, Pabst and Piscator. Béla Balázs mentioned the film in his "Build an International Union of Revolutionary Cinema" as proof that it was "possible to make use of old reviews by rearranging them so as to bring out the necessary viewpoint. "The opening performance provoked scandal by showing a cleverly cut newsreel: shots and scenes which had all been contained in old UFA newsreels were here combined in such manner that they suddenly lost their political innocence and assumed an inflammatory character. The police prohibited this devilish juggler's trick in utter disregard of the defendants' objection that the incriminating newsreel was nothing but an assemblage of unchanged material." Those films that were made by others and that are approved by the censors can be re-edited to show the real social sense, the real relationships." Piscator had used archival footage and newsreels, in conjunction with original footage, in his theatrical productions. He had put such films to use in *Hoppla, Such is Life!* when "a small group led by Victor Blum was in and out of the archives of the big film companies all the time," but he ran into trouble with his next play *Rasputin*: "The directors of the archives had, in the meantime, seen the use to which their inherently harmless film clips were going to be put." Assistance came from the use of pieces from Esfir Shub's *The Fall of the Romanov Dynasty.*

At Piscator's apartment one fall evening in 1928 Harry Kessler met Brecht for the first time. Afterwards he moved over to speak with Herzfelde who—". . . once again discussed with George Grosz and myself his notion of making a film solely from shots of actual events. Grosz was opposed to the idea or, at least very critical. "It can make an interesting document, but reality as such does not interest me. You see, I am what you may call an artistic person and what I aspire to is the fabulous. The camera can achieve all sorts of interesting snippets, but never the magical effects of draughtsmanship."

Esfir Shub had another opinion on the capacity for "interesting snippets" to achieve "magical effects". For her there was the "magic power of scissors in the hands of an individual who understands montage." Some explanation of all this magic has to be ventured into because it bears upon a source of Heartfield's popularity.

Heartfield hoped photomontage would stimulate a critical presence of the working class through cultural production. As with photography, few technical skills were needed and reasonable access to the medium was assured. A mobilization of a widespread production was, however, a difficult desire at best. In lieu of, and not exclusive from, a mobilized production is the potentially critical value inhered in the correspondence of the labor made evident within the photomontage and the "little labors" of daily life, i.e., a resonance of material practices—the cutting-up of photographs and the sustaining labors usually found outside normative (at that time, industrial and male) labor. These sustaining labors often do not elicit products but engender states. A photomontage invites by example a (phantom) application of these labors to an object of representation and ideology and thus, an invitation to develop a state of skepticism and criticality. In this respect a pair of Shub's "magic scissors" inhabits the everyday much more so that the skilled hands of Grosz. Even if Heartfield's photomontages almost never related thematically to everyday life, they did so materially almost every time.

It's at this intersection of intellectual and manual labor where signification is rendered palpable and a handling by the viewers is encouraged; the photomontage's tactilism in the context of photojournalism sets up an homology between the labors of physical and ideological construction at the same time as serving as a model of transgression. The flip side of an artistic process which, as has been stated above, has structured a pre-emptive consumption into the process of production is a consumption which contains an unusually active, productive component. This functions not only as a source of appeal, as an exemplar resourcefulness within the confines of daily experience, but also as a potentially critical process parallel to daily resistances of a "micro-political" nature. It invites holding the dominant sleight-of-hand at arms length, the distance necessary for cutting something up, to make a practice of customizing customary practice.

This concurrence of labors is determined entirely by the characteristics of the material, which is first of all marked by the concurrence of physicality and sociality. All artistic processes must begin with raw material. Mass media qualifies as raw material by virture of its violent reduction of communication and experience, actual and potential, past the reductions all cultural performances and products must work through. It is sufficiently reified to be handled physically in a manner of the traditional physical materials of the arts: wood, paint, metal, etc. Traditional materials, however, go through a transformation from physical to psychical whereas mass media starts out as psychical; its molecules are populated. What grain holds for wood something on the order of language would hold for mass media.

All materials resist an application of labor. Overcoming the resistances of the physical (technical) demands of mass media as raw material is relatively insignificant. A large number of tools are in fact contained in the material already, say, the lighting and sound equipment of a studio. This has the positive result of providing access to staff and equipment to individuals not institutionally or financially connected, at the cost, of course, of not being able to fundamentally change the lighting, sound, etc. Piscator's *Hoopla. Such is Life!* was plagued by the disruptive intersplicing of old and new historical film and original film footage—in the manner recordings from different rooms or recording equipment will contrast. Such limitations can be circumvented by creating segues with staged footage, titling or subtitling or, in Heartfield's case, by drawing and painting (unfortunately, in conjunction with his anti-expressionism Heartfield held painting and other plastic means in check, limiting the capacity to depict fully the viscerality of barbarism). When it got down to it, all Heartfield needed was a head.

Even the tools outside the material proper are primarily the reapplied instruments of editing and revision. If, as Marx would often quote, "Of you the story is told" then this can be seen as a simple editing for accuracy, reeling in a ghost writer more comfortable with science fiction than political biography. The most cumbersome technical demands arise from the need for a reasonably coordinated expanse of raw material, archives or whatever—how

118

to categorize and associate while letting the unlikely brush up against one another. Yet even this has necessity in a totally social basis of the resistance of ideology to be waiting bundled and babbling at the front doorstep or encapsulated inside a clenched fist. It is to be found, barring accidents, only over large expanses, which themselves are small components of the inundation of the mass media, the inundation being the absolute locus of its politics (this long story must be cut short).

The sociality of mass media as raw material moves the figurative dialogue between producer and material, which ensues anytime an initial artistic mark is made, toward a literal dialogue. With the former, the physical material is infused with socialness through a tension with the producer's conception of its final form. The latter is preconceived, already having taken a form committed to an existence autonomous from the new producer.

The figurative dialogue within most artistic processes is one with the person the artist knows best, one on the socially acceptable side of those who, talking to themselves on city streets, also understand an audience to be a crucial presence. The near literal dialogue with mass media as raw material is with an "other" the producer must come to know intimately for, unlike the predictable and surmountable resistances of physical material, it is in each case unique. The task of familiarization is aided by the other's immobility. No matter whether in all other circumstances power may be exercised with impunity by the other, here it is helpless. The producer uses this occasion to fully embrace the material, to listen to it to a degree surpassing deep respect in actual dialogue (consider how grueling this could be, paying due respect to a George Will, golf, Jane Fonda, Kermit the Frog, soaps, human interest, etc.). At this point another member joins the conversation, the previously "mute other" that has been begging to be born from the other's "pregnance with the opposite."

The whole productive process must be geared to coax the mute other to speak candidly; it is here where the greatest resistance of the material is to be found. (The stalemate at this point can be compared to a session where the analysand joins the analyst in his/her pregnant silences.) All the critical and poetical resources of the producer, and those not previously in the possession of the producer, must be called up because, although there may be a pregnance with the opposite, the delivery can be extremely difficult. It is, afterall, a delivery into destruction. The mute other may be the harbinger of truth but it is also the violence repressed from appearance. Its release signals the other's self-inflicted hurt and demise.

Mimikry

"He imitates his subjects in order to insert the crowbar of his hate into the finest joints of their posture."

—Walter Benjamin on Karl Krauss

Mimikry, as a specific instance of mimesis where what is being mimicked participates, was best attempted (but never realized) by Piscator. According to Brecht, Piscator could not get proper permission for an actor to impersonate the former emperor Kaiser Wilhelm II so he went to Wilhelm directly with an actor's contract in hand. And of course was rebuffed.

His self-portrayal in a Piscator production would have been an historical pinnacle of candor and confession, let alone a definitive moment in the history of realism. There would have been no doubt that it was the Kaiser playing himself but not being himself. It would have been more than an imitation but nothing like him. Piscator would have been the first to direct an actor in the destruction of his true social role and his own self.

Mimikry can be discussed in the abstract in its relation to a hoax of total simulation. In such a hoax, the imitator (or mime) is poured into and grafted upon the mold and behavior of the original. Any protrusive discrepancies are tucked and filed down to seamlessness (seme-lessness). All evidence of sources, labor and other histories, and moments of the object or act are submerged well within the reified norms of the original.

In stopping short of hoax, mimikry brings corresponding and contradictory aspects of both the original and mime to the fore, in the manner of modernist self-reflexivity. Unlike the bulk of artistic modernism, however, mimikry reflects back not only upon its own act but brings the social existence of the original, with which it is inseparable, into scrutiny. The complex resultant movements between original and mime (disguise, confusion, ambivalence, discovery, revelation, among others) constitute the true elements orchestrated within the tactic of mimikry.

Mimikry is a tactic, not a strategy. Although it may function oppositionally with unusual competence (largely from beginning with full access to the affect of the original) it may also function, as with hoax, within the problematic of the original to recuperate the potential resistance of the mime. The original's centrality and beneficient tolerance are momentarily demonstrated in a trade-off for the recognition of the mime's past and future impotence. This recuperation by the dominant society is particularly virulent, in this case, because it presents in an instant a social process of recuperation which normally is achieved over the long-term.

Recuperation is the topic of Heartfield's 19 April 1934 photomontage "Mimikry". Propaganda Minister Goebbels, his legs greatly shortened, stands in the seat of power in order to adorn Hitler with Marx's facial hair, covering Hitler's own distinct shave. Hitler holds a Labor Day medallion bearing, in relief, a revealing ensemble of symbols. The text reads:

> After all the efforts to introduce Nazi ideas into the workers' community were found to have been unsuccessful, Goebbels has convinced the Führer that when he addresses workers in the future he should wear a Karl Marx beard.
>
> Press report of 8 April 1934: "This year's May Day posters of the national Labor Front will show the head of Goethe, the eagle with the swastika and the Bolshevik symbol, the hammer and sickle, so as to win over for the regime any workers tending toward opposition."

This maneuver came while the Nazis were ruling and the opposition was illegal. Inversely, much of Nazi symbology was originally generated in opposition to the range of socialisms during Weimar: the Nazi red flag, new words filling proletarian songs, antibourgeois slogans accompanying nationalist calls for revolution, etc. The very name of the NSDAP, National Socialist German Workers Party, had "socialist" and "workers" taken from the socialist tradition to which the majority of Weimar workers had allegiance. After 1933 the Nazis funded an imitation A-I-Z named A-B-Z, *Arbeiter Bild Zeitung*—Bild and Illustrierte being synonymous in this context. (A Dutch workers paper, unable to afford the copper plate rotogravure of A-I-Z, settled for copper-colored ink to achieve its more sympathetic ends.) A typical recuperation: Goebbels once commented while watching the ascending smoke and flames of a book burning, "Here the intellectual stands next to the worker; a whole people has risen up!"(sic)

The premier Nazi fabrication was the 1 September 1939 attack on the Gleiwitz radio station at the Polish border where SS men dressed in Polish uniforms killed German prisoners already sentenced to execution. A matter of hours later Hitler used this theater production in order to invade Poland and christen WWII. The state manufacture of such pretexts is still commonplace today.

Heartfield's use of mimikry within an oppositional practice began with the recourse to photomontage during WWI. By mimicking nationalist postcards the photomontages were able to pass by the wartime censors. In the same respect, Herzfelde "took cover" during WWI behind the imprimatur of a youth magazine to publish *Neue Jugend*. The point, apart from a conveniently clever name, was to blow the cover on the war and nationalism, to showcase contemporary writing and to find a carrier of that communication, not to level a critique upon the carrier. This form of mimikry, then, was primarily a matter of distribution and not reception. It can be found again on the other side of Weimar in the resistance during the early years of the Third Reich. To introduce oppositional information into Germany "life and death cleverness" was employed. Gustav Regler in his memoirs recounts how pamphlets—

> . . . were disguised in the most ingenious fashion, some being tucked away in seed-packets such as are sold in Germany. On the outside were pictures of vegetables and flowers. The colors pleased the eye, but the producers of this illegal seed were not so innocent as to suppose that Hitler's police would be deterred by this brightness from looking inside the packets. Therefore they were filled with real seeds, together with the usual instructions:
> "To be sown in March or April under glass and planted out in May. Height about three feet. Blooms throughout the summer in various colors."
> Further information was given, but in the middle of the text an unknown voice would speak of Hitler's evil deeds and call for the sowing of other seed. . . . packets of shampoo were distributed and amid the scented powder lurked the leaflet proclaiming that Germany reaked of blood.[60]

Another method included placing text within packages of photographic paper—they could not be opened for inspection without inconvenience or exposure. A version of the *Brown Book on Nazi Terror* was inserted into mass distributed classics, Goethe's *Hermann und Dorothea* and Schiller's *Wallerstein*; while the journal *Oktober* was printed under the cover of *Modern Architecture*. Text was also camouflaged in film reviews of the type distributed by the thousands at movie houses.

Among the latter was the review, "The Sign of the Cross: A Cecil de Mille—Paramount Production." It began describing the persecution of Christians during Rome, a thinly veiled parallel made famous by "inner emigration" writers, then broke abruptly into a message countering the Nazi account of the Reichstag fire.

> A reward of 20,000 Marks was set by the government for evidence tending to clear up the fire which took place in the Reichstag on the evening of February 27 [1933]. Whoever will read the following carefully can easily earn this reward.

This pamphlet, which at one time found its way to all the work stations in an entire factory, went on to name Goering as the cul-

IM ZEICHEN

DES KREUZES

Ein C. d. Mille-Film der Paramount

prit and to compare the Reichstag fire with "the fire to come."

> In spite of everything![Trotz Alledem!]/Forward to the German Red
> October!/*The Red Conflagration Cannot Be Stamped Out!*/Many a
> worker has fallen/Since Hitler came to reign./However, he cannot
> extinguish/The towering bright Red flame./His murder and his arson
> tales/Let him each day repeat;/Yet we shall never surrender/Nor ever
> shall know defeat./Communism lives!

Such rhetorical maladies, which hung over from legal times,
combined with the growing distance to domestic German realities
from which they were penned plus the crude means by which they
were produced made for frustratingly ineffectual resistance literature. "I arrived in time to hear the last words of a young man who
had been reporting on conditions in Germany. When he had
finished speaking he produced one of the leaflets from his pocket
and tossed it with a gesture of utter disdain at the feet of the high
official. 'We've been circulating that for months,' he said. 'We've
gone with you so far, but now we're sick of it. For God's sake, who
do you expect to convince? Who are you aiming at?' He pointed
with his foot at the pamphlet and concluded with a devastating
finality: 'We aren't going to risk our lives any longer for that
crap!'"[61]

In this context of resistance literature A-I-Z must have been
refreshing. Although methods of mimikry were not employed for
distribution reduced copies were introduced into Germany printed
on thin paper in order to be carried secretively on the person. The
cover of one carried Heartfield's photomontage "Mimikry." On
one occasion, distribution of Heartfield's work inside Nazi Germany occurred in an unexpected manner.

> One time Himmler was forced to confiscate and destroy the latest
> issue of his own newspaper, *Das Schwarze Korps*. Reimann. . . had
> published one of my montages with an agitation article attacking
> me. It must have scared them. However, it evidently pleased the
> Berliners a great deal because the issue sold out very quickly. Him-
> mler was only able to recover a few copies of this issue of his paper.

In circumstances of strict censorship, such as WWI and the Nazi
period, mimikry was used simply to gain access to a public, at
times, apparently *any* public. A packet of cucumber seeds will
pass through even the most repressive regime unencumbered. No

outstanding need for a critique of the representations of seeds or garden vegetables exists. In bourgeois democratic times where it is usually not necessary to circumvent a censor at a bottleneck of distribution, mimikry circumvents conventions of self-censorship bottlenecking reception. In this attempt it is put into a position where a critique of the carrier may also be delivered. When perusing through the pages of an illustrated weekly the photojournalistic-look of Heartfield's work is anticipated. In the wake of experiencing Heartfield's work the photomontage-look of photojournalism may come to be anticipated. One the other hand, critical imperatives in, say, a Grosz or Kollwitz work are signaled well ahead of time and are in no position to level residual critiques on modes of representation within the mass media.

Ideally, a Heartfield work will be apprehended for what it is only after entering it. There must be, of course, a disclosure of the fact that it is a work of mimikry for the dual critique to be accomplished and to pull-up short of hoax; mimikry's deception discloses the deception of the original. The delay until disclosure in most Heartfield photomontages is miniscule. The important distinguishing factor is that the entrance into the work does not require a suspension of belief or alteration in patterns of expectation. Mimikry under militarized scrutiny requires greatly delayed disclosure. In other times, the delay can be as momentary or prolonged as is tactically necessary.

A contemporary of Heartfield, Marinus Jacob Kjelgaard, produced over 200 photomontages for the liberal French "grand literary illustrated weekly" *Marianne* between 1930 and 1940. A 4 October 1939 Kjelgaard photomontage showing Hitler painting the exterior of a tavern (Hitler at one time was a house painter) is captioned, "The world would live in peace if each worked at his job."[62] The photomontage approaches a naturalism more engulfing and thus of longer delay than anything in Heartfield's output. It still discloses itself within its own frame. It could have pushed toward elimination of all such signals but because of the status of Hitler at that time, having invaded Poland and all, it could not have failed to disclose itself no matter how far it was pushed. Social phenomena of lesser prominence are open to closer mimikry. Other aspects of mimikry are here demonstrated by recent examples.

Recent Mimikry

1. Oppositional mimikry is hardly limited to photomontage. One instance by the West German artist/lawyer Klaus Staeck, though he is certainly the contemporary inheritor of Heartfield's practice of photomontage, is not a photomontage. A 1972 poster composed solely of type, it mimicked an election poster of a right-wing German party. It read, *The rich must get richer still. So vote CDU.* "A variation of this was made which said *Die Mieten müssen steigen. [Rents must go up.] Wählt Christdemokratisch.* Both forms of the poster were also produced as stickers and postcards: by 19 November a total of 300,000 had been printed and distributed." Legal injunctions, 10 in all, were brought against the poster. A Superior District Court cited Staeck for the imitation of the name of the CDU. To adjust the mimikry to the letter of the law, "the words *Deshalb CDU* [Thus CDU] were altered to *wählt Christdemokratish* [Vote Christian Democrat]. "

> Thanks to the extensive publicity, which was, of course, assisted by the CDU-instituted legal proceedings, all the national newspapers were able to propogate the poster slogan in the course of their reports. In the local press alone the slogan had been repeated at least 40 times. In the meantime over 130 newspaper articles on the subject had appeared.[63]

Further exposure occurred on television and radio. Because the poster's distribution satisfactorily occurred within the intended terrain, known in the business as "outdoor art", the exposure within other regimes of media was frosting on the cake.

Hans Haacke's "American Cyanamid", an adept use of mimikry, had difficulty gaining the same degree of distribution. It showed a painting of a "Breck shampoo girl" familiar to anyone who had read womens magazines in the United States. Haacke's text read:

> AMERICAN CYANAMID is the parent of BRECK Inc., maker of the shampoo which keeps the Breck Girl's hair clean, shining and beautiful.
>
> AMERICAN CYANAMID does more for women. It knows: "we really don't run a health spa."
>
> And therefore those of its female employees of child-bearing age who are exposed to toxic substances are now given a choice.

They can be reassigned to a possibly lower paying job within the company. They can leave if there is no opening. Or they can have themselves sterilized and stay in their old job.

Four West Virginia women chose sterilization.

AMERICAN CYANAMID. . . WHERE WOMEN HAVE A CHOICE.

In an interview Haacke recounts, "I offered it as a poster design to the Oil, Chemical and Atomic Workers Union and the Coalition for Reproductive Rights. Eventually word came that people didn't quite understand my mock ad, and therefore it wasn't done. The first time it got large exposure was in *The Village Voice*. I was quite happy about that but that was five or six years after I actually did the piece."[64]

2. A media afterlife for some instances of mimikry is absolutely necessary because their street life can be brief. This is particularly true for the burgeoning practice of billboard corrections. Three Seattle artists collectively known in their anonymity as SSS reworked a billboard; their efforts were down in a day. However, in its media afterlife it was released on wire photo gaining a national and some international attention.

The original billboard had read "Hollywood Bowled Over By Kent III Taste," displaying a pack of cigarettes to the side. SSS mimicked this in exacting typeface to read "Hollywood Bowled Over by Neutron Bomb!" Over the cigarette pack was placed a large Hollywood glossy portrait-like drawing of Ronald Reagan. This was a response to the Reagan Administration announcement it was planning to put the bomb back into production. The idea was conceived the day of the announcement. The billboard was up two days later. In a January 1982 interview SSS commented upon their tactic.

It's important to make statements that are not like a lot of political posters, which are immediately identifiable. For most people, once they have recognized a political poster, they've catalogued it away and disposed of the idea. But taking a statement out of any sensible context and putting it into a billboard challenges the whole communicative element in people's minds and leaves them vulnerable.[65]

An Australian organization was founded to support the efforts of that country's billboard graffitists (some of the billboards employed mimikry). "Graffiti has traditionally been a cheap and effective medium of self-expression for those who do not have access to the commercial media. The added dimension of using billboards is that ads can be turned against themselves, so that advertisers fund their own 'demotions' (anti-promotions)." The group is known by the acronym for Billboard Utilizing Graffitists Against Unhealthy Promotions, BUGA UP ("bugger up" in Australianese means to "screw up").

Being audaciously public adds a third level of critique to commentary and the critique of the carrier; persistant legal transgression critiques the property relations nestled into the communicative and legal apparatuses. Most significantly, it makes law *per se* observable as a representation of class rule and market dictates and puts this representation on par with advertising and spectacle.

Looking back over about forty court cases, BUGA UP activist Peter King wrote:

> Several defenses have been tried. The most fruitful of these has been the "defense of necessity", which claims that a minor wrong was committed to prevent a much more serious one—such as harm to people who might otherwise have believed that smoking and drinking would improve their sex life. BUGA UP has called witnesses to testify that the promotion in question was indeed unhealthy. Expert witnesses have also been used to argue that the billboard was not damaged but in fact improved; the alterations enhanced its truthfulness and transformed it into a unique work of art.
>
> Although legally unsuccessful, these arguments have attracted media attention and won the movement wide-spread sympathy. So far, three out of four graffitists have been found guilty; penalties have ranged from a stern reprimand to a fine of about two hundred dollars. From this point of view, civil disobedience has proved to be an extremely cost-effective way of raising public consciousness.[66]

3. The West German journalist Günter Wallraff incorporated mimikry to elaborate an oppositional *sting*, resulting in his most famous article "The Coup Merchants".[67]

Posing as an unspecified but "understood" West German operative he infiltrated the right-wing paramilitary ranks of the Democratic Movement for the Liberation of Portugal (MDLP). Wallraff tells about a meeting of MDLP officers he and his translator attended:

I describe our assignment, saying that we are representatives of a right-wing German organization who have been sent here in strict secrecy to get a picture of the situation for ourselves and then to make arrangements for financial aid and the supply of arms. In the discussion it becomes clear that the MDLP is planning a coup before the Presidential elections in May or June. This coup will re-establish a right-wing dictatorship in Portugal, with all active left-wing forces liquidated.

There is a lot of whiskey being poured out and we are encouraged to drink as much as we want. After this meeting I am absolutely shattered. Constantly having to keep up this act. The nervous tension. Being forced to join in with a happy laugh when someone drinks to the killing of political 'opponents.' We are accompanied back to the four-star Vermar hotel on the seafront. After that I lose control. It is a kind of nervous breakdown, with prolonged bursts of crying.

This is a brazen brand of mimikry; immersion in the despised material is not safely mediated through representations. Likewise, anonymity is an exaggeratedly active one; unlike most mimikry which deals with representation and myth this is action and ritual. Like certain other instances, however, it did lead to the unexpected where the material produces on its own, in this case, to a meeting with General Antonio de Spinola, former President of Portugal, architect of the coup and its would-be inheritor. Wallraff invited him to meet his "president" in Düsseldorf and Spinola accepted. In describing the meeting at the airport on 25 March 1976 Wallraff notes parenthetically:

(The scene which follows is so unreal, the kind of musical comedy situation you find in poor German films, that it would have been dismissed as pure invention and utter exaggeration if it had not been authentic and proved to be true. This is a case where reality outstrips the author's powers of imagination.)

After being unable to find someone willing to play the part of the West German president, a friend is finally convinced, not very long before the dinner where the formal meeting is to take place. The "president" arrives in a limo, carries a briefcase, nods knowingly. He gives Wallraff, who is wired for sound, the powers of negotiation. The information gained scuttled the planned coup in Portugal and exposed connections between the MDLP and forces in Germany, including Franz Josef Strauss.

On 7 April Wallraff held a press conference in Bonn in which he revealed Spinola's plans and the Spinola-Strauss contacts. The next day the popular magazine *Stern* published a Wallraff story that again detailed the events. On 12 April Wallraff was featured on the television news magazine "Panorama". He offered viewers tangible proof of the facts: portions of taped conversations with Spinola, weapons lists and documents supplied by Spinola or his confidants, and photographs of the Spinola-Wallraff meeting in Düsseldorf.

4. In Poland, the fall of 1983, the government broadcasted an audio tape of Lech Walesa telling his brother to invest one million dollars in Western prize money in an interest-bearing Vatican bank account. Walesa said the tape was of a conversation that never took place but was instead pieced together from many fragments.

Solidarity retaliated with a tape of their own but one that did not attempt to deceive. It was produced from the infamous 13 December 1981 broadcast of General Wojciech Jaruzelski declaring martial law. In a simple inversion they had the general, in an unusual moment of candor, saying "Citizens, men and women, the following in a nutshell is the truth about martial law. There have come into effect, or shortly will come into effect, laws making a mockery of the principles of morality and justice. . . There are not now, and will never be, independent, self-governing trade unions, democracy and self-government; let no one at home or abroad harbor any such illusions even for a moment. . . There will be a new period of life in our homeland. We intend to consolidate it effectively, to consolidate the crime which threatens the life, limb and property of our citizens, and also [to consolidate] speculation, bribery and tax fraud."[68] On the same tape there were musical selections and a cut-up of Deputy Prime Minister Mieczyslaw Rakowski, who was found saying, "I repeat once more, that it was the authorities who destroyed Solidarity, this beautiful idea, this beautiful, healing movement."

5. One of the most successful single instances of mimikry recently was an audio tape created by members of the British anarchist rock group CRASS. In an Associated Press interview, band member Andy Palmer explained the action:

We took extracts from speeches by Thatcher and Reagan, put them together with some telephone noises over the top and distributed it anonymously on the continent. A Dutch journalist took it to the States where it ended up in the State Department in Washington, who promptly issued a statement saying that they felt it was part of the "Soviet disinformation campaign". Subsequent to that, the (London) Sunday *Times* got ahold of it and, acting purely as a mouthpiece for the State Department, printed an article entitled "How the KGB Fools the West's Press."

The tape was first released in Holland in May 1983. It submerges a crude cutting job under noises sounding as though it had been intercepted over the mid-Atlantic. The U.S. State Department issued a written statement saying, "From the drift of the tape, the evident purpose was to cause problems for Mrs. Thatcher by blaming her for the sinking of the British destroyer Sheffield [during the Falkland Islands invasion], and also for us by stirring trouble on the INF [Intermediate Range Nuclear Forces] issue." The tape lifts from a 22 November 1982 Reagan speech on nuclear armaments to have him say, "In conflict, we will launch missiles on allies for effective limitation of the Soviet Union." The State Department said, "This type of activity fits the pattern of fabrications circulated by the Soviet KGB, although usually they involve fake documents rather than tapes."

Eight months later, on 8 January 1984, CRASS announced that they had manufactured the tape and the scheme. Palmer, "It is a hoax. We intended it to be a hoax. . . If the State is using methods to pull the wool over our eyes then it seems fair enough to use the same methods to try and expose the truth." The method here was not primarily a mimikry of Thatcher and Reagan, that is, a mimikry immanent to the work, but an opportune orchestration of a compliant self-mimikry from the U.S. State Department. The pervasive knee-jerk anti-Sovietism in the Administration was predictable enough to tap into from clear across the ocean—a trans-Atlantic puppetry utilizing U.S. "intelligence". The State Department had, afterall, applied Science; language experts went as far as determining "that the author was not a native Dutch speaker."

The AP reporter, after being surprised that the tape's authors were unrepentent, asked CRASS if they would put out more tapes. Palmer replied by throwing back the type of rhetoric proffered at the State Department: "We will continue working in the same fields."

6. In 1967 Paul Krassner, editor of *The Realist,* wrote an article entitled, "The Parts That Were Left Out of the Kennedy Book."[69] In it he claimed that the magazine was privy to a photostatic copy of the original manuscript of William Manchester's book, *The Death of a President.* This manuscript was said to reveal portions of the book that had been excised in later stages. Gore Vidal had already "explained why Jacqueline Kennedy will never relate to Lyndon Johnson. During that tense journey from Dallas to Washington after the assassination, she inadvertently walked in on him as he was standing over the casket of his predecessor and chuckling. This disclosure was the talk of London but not a word was mentioned here."

The manuscript in the possession of *The Realist* went further, quoting Jackie describing the entire scene she witnessed in Air Force One. Lyndon Johnson was not only chuckling "he was literally fucking my husband in the throat. In the bullet wound in the front of his throat. He reached a climax and dismounted. I froze. The next thing I remember, he was being sworn in as the new President."

Krassner documented the repurcussions from the article. The whole idea had come from the addition of one letter to "necrophilia" to read "neckrophilia". The mimikry employed launched it into national attention. In a telephone conversation with someone posing as William Manchester, Krassner said: "Well, I had to establish verisimilitude. When Jonathan Swift wrote his "Modest Proposal" he didn't say, 'Hey folks, I'm only kidding, I don't really mean that we can solve both the famine and overpopulation by eating newborn babies.' It wouldn't have had the same impact." The tactic could also be rationalized by another source not as canonized in literature as Swift.

> . . . One of LBJ's favorite jokes is about a popular Texas sheriff running for reelection. His opponents have been trying unsuccessfully to think of a good campaign issue to use against him. Finally one man suggests spreading "a rumor that he fucks pigs." Another protests, "You know he doesn't do that." "I know," says the first man, "but let's make the son-of-a-bitch deny it."

Johnson nor the White House commented on the article. Nevertheless, the tactical effect described in the LBJ quip came about in a UPI syndicated article by Merriman Smith who wrote, "The incident, of course, never took place."

7. The two strains of left and non-conformist modernism, as distinguished by Breton, met in the French Situationists, a small but influential post-war group most associated with the activities of May 68. The importance of their cultural thought lies in its non-exclusivity of the outwardly activist orientation of the left modernists and the radicalization of subjectivity of the non-conformists. It was not necessarily a matter of reconciling the two, for which they would have had large claim upon everyone's attention, as depriving either an exclusive status as principle, subsuming them instead in a program exemplified by the Situationist re-

versal of the Surrealist "Poetry in the service of revolution!" to "Revolution in the service of poetry" (in accord with the *homo aestheticus* anticipated by Marx which would develop in the period after the end of the pre-history marked by class rule).

The Situationists' concept covering reversals within cultural tactics is *detournement,* first theorized by Guy Debord and Gil Wolman in 1956.[70] As a mode of symbolic reversal it is restricted, like mimikry, to redirecting the meanings of pre-existing cultural entities. Within these bounds it is incredibly expansive, considering there is nothing in the spectacle and very little entering into communication that does not qualify as culture. A range was covered from detourning historical inheritances, wherein oppositional functioning was either restored or instilled for present-day consumption, to a project of negation with a definite bohemian caste, which was seen as predisposing generative processes of working class affirmation. The latter project was postponed, in the Sit scenario, to a later stage of their optimistically perceived "transitory period," nevertheless, detournement was a "first step toward a *literary communism.*"

While the practice of detournement has often been equated with its subversive street actions, Debord and Wolman's formulation, when it doesn't degenerate into precious incorporation of detourned "elements" in Lettriste collages, favors the indoor sports of the intellect.

> It is. . . necessary to conceive of a parodic-serious stage where the accumulation of detourned elements, far from aiming at arousing indignation or laughter by alluding to some original work, will express our *indifference* toward a meaningless and forgotten original, and concern itself with rendering a certain *sublimity.*

Along these lines, they are quick to cite the precedent of Lautreàmont. His own reversals began with the adoption of his name from a novel by Eugene Sue, apropos Herzfeld's Anglicization, and reached methodological proportions in his use of *plagarism.* In *Poèsies* he hung his words on the frame of Pascal's *Pensèes* (as well as La Rochefoucauld, Vauvenargues and even the Lautreàmont of *Maldoror*), "correcting" the citations in due course of his own philosophical medley—not totally dissimilar to Grosz and Heartfield's "Corrected Picasso" and "Corrected Rousseau" but probably closer to espresso coreto, a corrected espresso accomplished by the addition of grappa.

Since cultural categories are themselves reversible, detournement migrated freely among numerous forms and media; among them film was privileged in concept if not in action. Wolman and Debord proposed a corrected D. W. Griffith; it differs from compilation films in that it wouldn't necessarily use film's segmentation to aid the adaptation.

> . . . we can observe that Griffith's *Birth of a Nation* is one of the most important films in the history of the cinema because of its wealth of new contributions. On the other hand, it is a racist film and therefore absolutely does not merit being shown in its present form. But its total prohibition could be seen as regretable from the point of view of the secondary, but potentially worthier, domain of the cinema. It would be better to *detourn* it as a whole, without necessarily even altering the montage, by adding a soundtrack that made a powerful denunciation of the horrors of imperialist war and of the activities of the Ku Klux Klan, which are continuing in the United States even now.

The more familiar form of detournement had a classical moment at the University of California at Berkeley, May 1972, orchestrated by the Situationist-inspired group Point Blank, as described by Tom Ward.

> Several thousand copies of the *Last Daily Cal* were surreptitiously deposited at all the campus distribution points where somnabulant students routinely picked up the dreary rag it parodied. The front page revealed why this was to be the *last* issue—complete with a letter from the Chancellor "thanking" the staff for having been such well-behaved liberals—while inside was a scathing assault on some cozy assumptions of the Berkeley scene. This "intervention" certainly had the desired, disorienting effect. Not only was the paper read with more avid curiousity than usual, but the "real" *Daily Cal* staff was compelled to make an embarrassed public denial—which, of course, was feeble and too late.[71]

Whereas this example belongs easily to oppositional mimikry, detournement as a whole does not, the main reason being that in the concept of detournement "elements" of pre-existing cultural phenomena are admitted as satisfactory carriers of the tactic

136

whereas mimikry requires a presence of a total entity, where the constituent elements (and constitution) are evident, if not the surrounding contexts. The generally preferable quality of mimikry lies in the critical way it directs memory. Where ". . . the main force of a detournement is directly related to the conscious or vague recollection of the original contexts of the elements. . ." the main force of mimikry is directly related to the mnemonic effect on the future contexts of the total entity. Elements require a "re-collected" whole for their individual significance and they may not necessarily appear in further manifestations of their parent whole—the whole is primarily contingent upon its contexts. An invocation of the whole from the beginning, as in mimikry, relieves the burden of its retrospective construction. The detournement of elements thus looks back and invokes to inform its own act while mimikry arrives complete to disrupt other acts, a criticality which stigmatizes and problematizes the future.

The systemic exclusion of other voices from the U.S. mass media has made it so there is nothing with a regular national reach that does not ultimately participate in immiseration and murder; the phenomena which participate more directly, say, evangelical programming or presidential addresses, should not distract from an inspection of all varieties of hegemonic glue. Such saturation makes a selection of an object of critique easy in that anything can be selected and interrogated for, although a conviction may be difficult to obtain, an indictment is guaranteed. The artistic process or, rather, artistic prosecution requires a singular, unitary concentration because of such widespread guilt. All variety of mass media phenomena have received just this type of attention in academic journals over the last ten years or so but they have neither been translated nor initiated on a commensurate scale within cultural products and peformances. (How much more trenchant the performances of an academic conference where critiques are delivered through the form of or actual objects of critique.) The unitary focus within mimikry sets limits to the lateral mobility of detournement's referencing of elements and mitigates against at least three resultant pitfalls not explicitly mitigated within the detournement of elements. 1) Because the element invoked relies on a relationship to an absent whole, only those who have knowledge of this prior relationship will understand the inversion of the element, therefore the danger of degeneration to inside information, inside jokes. 2) Because so much is corrupt there exists a tendency to marshall a multitude of elements which give an appearance of an apprehension and delivery of complexity but whose only unity is found in the author's state of new found disgust. 3) The lateral movement of reference is also followed in search for a basis of critique, therefore the easy recourse in nostalgia, anachronisms, clichès, and all other moments where ridicule is confused with critique. Mimikry instead (1) comes equipped with a whole (to the extent mass media's closures ape totalities). It can supply all the background information, if not more, that was provided by the original in order to recreate an experience of the vernacular. With mimikry, the appearance of the whole has never been abdicated; the critique is both within and of appearance. 2) If a multitude of elements are to be invoked their most immediate relationship is with the fatuously constituted whole of the original. Thus any lateral movement toward eclecticism is bounded toward depth. If there is any condescending fear of the possibility for communication of adequate depth, a quick look at the formidable demands made upon vernacular and structural comprehension by advertisings or film trailers (a hyper-montage which makes Eisenstein look like slow motion) should allay such fear and open up the possibility of a negation of those forms, among many others, on the terrain of their seemingly infinite adaptations. 3) If historically regressive references are made within mimikry it is only because they have been made within the original. They therefore pre-exist as recuperations of the past and thus as objects of critique, not bases for critique. Although the critique must be historical it cannot fall back on a historical distancing which finds only the past ridiculous.

8. As should be obvious in most of these examples, mimikry was inseparable from the inordinantly wide distribution and attention received. The incursions were, however, momentary and for the most part through dominant mass media channels opposed or disinterested in the critiques presented. Thus, most incidents of recent mimikry are distinct from Heartfield's practice. Heartfield's incursions were protracted and the mass media channels in which he was based were supportive and were themselves suspended within a larger supportive socio-political context. He was promoted, not merely tolerated, within a competitive mass media

sphere during late-Weimar. This protracted oppositional stature was the result of large historical and societal factors which are not with us today. There's no reason to bemoan this interim absence too long, especially if it means belittling the acts of mimikry for succeeding, albeit momentarily, in such oppressive communicative conditions.

Simulation

"They had to put her back together in sections as if they were making a photomontage." —An old friend of Frida Kahlo speaking about the time following her accident.

Zeuxis, as the myth goes, wanted to create the perfect woman. He had been commissioned to create a sculpted image of Helen of Troy but trusted neither his imagination nor the beauty of any one model. He therefore chose attributes "from the five most beautiful maidens" living in the city of Crotona where the sculpture was to stand.

After Dziga Vertov was unable to pursue his first artistic desire to create aural works using sound montage (because adequate technology simply did not exist) he moved into film. Here he typified the modern day Zeuxis. Instead of chosing attributes from five maidens to organically form Helen, he chose from film fragments butted up against each other to mold his Adam-plus.

I am the cinema-eye. I create a man more perfect than Adam was created, I create thousands of different people from various preliminary sketches and plans.
I am the cinema-eye.
I take from one person the strongest and deftest hands, from another I take the stongest and swiftest legs, from a third the most beautiful and expressive head and I create a new, perfect man in a montage.[72]

Zeuxis was being resourceful; Vertov was testing the latitude of the new resources. Both could make their respective Helenistic claim to beauty or Adamic claim to the New Man because these claims would never be tested by the existence of real living individuals, Helen or Adam. It's safe when those fictionalized are dead, safer when they never lived, but dangerous when they're still around within ear and eye shot.

Roland Barthes in his essay "The Photographic Message" describes a photomontage that was never intended to disclose itself as such.

> A photograph given wide circulation in the American press in 1951 is reputed to have cost Senator Millard Tydings his seat; it showed the Senator in conversation with the Communist leader Earl Browder. In fact, the photograph had been faked, created by the artificial bringing together of the two faces. The methodological interest of trick effects is that they intervene without warning in the plane of denotation; they utilize the special credibility of the photograph—in order to pass off as a merely denoted message which is in reality heavily connoted; in no other treatment does connotation assume so completely the 'objective' mask of denotation. Naturally, signification is only possible to the extent that there is a stock of signs, the beginnings of a code. The signifier here is the conversational attitude of the two figures and it will be noted that this attitude becomes a sign only for a certain society, only given certain values. What makes the speakers' attitude the sign of a reprehensible familiarity is the tetchy anti-Communism of the American electorate; which is to say that the code of connotation is neither artificial (as in a true language) nor natural, but historical.[73]

Tydings and Browder are differentiated from Helen of Troy and Adam of Eden; the Americans were either already familiar or their identifications within the captions to the photo could be verified by eyewitness or compared to other photos. In terms of simulation, the Tydings/Browder photomontage is primitive, despite its reputed success. An appeal to more sophisticated manichaeanisms than "tetchy anti-Communism" becomes a bigger bill to fill. Once out of a binary ideology a more than binary paste-up job is required. It's no longer satisfactory to rely solely upon the "exceptional power of denotation" attendant upon photography; gesture and speech are glaringly absent. Once these are technologically available a new era of artifice will be inaugurated.

In the Tydings/Browder photograph the constituent elements are two simple heads which add up to a social situation. The heads in themselves are singular entities unfabricated by other constituent elements. In a more advanced form the elements of a single head

could be synthesized and plastically orchestrated. Given motion, a twitch fixing into an arch at the top toe of a crow's foot alongside the left eye could accompany, given speech, a degenerating inflectionary curve at the end of an exclamatory phrase. The former might have been taken from film stock twelve years ago, the latter gleaned from a video of the previous week. The result, along with numerous other components, would form a talking head in, say, a relatively prosaic moment.

This would still be dependent upon a large sampling of accumulated pre-existent material. As such, it will be superceded by a capacity for the generation of material interpolated within and extrapolated upon pre-existing material to create what might be needed but absent. Sophistication will be defined by how small a sample is needed to elicit a simulation of potentially infinite articulation. Auditorily it will be the act of writing with another person's speech; visually, the melding of puppetry and life. Biological existence will no longer be required for a person to act.

How this capacity for ultimate animation will be greeted is impossible to determine. That it will be greeted is certain, understanding that it is an immeasurably less complex problem than artificial intelligence (intelligence, or a reasonable facsimile *in vivo*, must be supplied to the simulation). Mimikry now relies upon an aesthetic and fantastic enactment of the collapse of the mime into the original for its potential criticality: "if so-and-so was mimicked so effectively this time, how am I to know the next time whether he or she are not actual artifice?" With total simulation this skepsis will confront the possibility of never being able to discern one way or the other. If a generalized skepsis will arise, or whether that will matter, remains to be seen. An expanded oppositional politics of artifice will be required to influence the outcome.

NOTES

[1] Arthur Garfield Hays, *City Lawyer*. New York, 1942.

[2] Hans Magnus Enzensberger, *The Consciousness Industry*. New York, 1974.

[3] Wieland Herzfelde, "The Curious Merchant from Holland"; *Harper's*. Nov. 1943. Other Herzfelde cited from: *Unterwegs. Blätter aus fünfzig Jahren*. Berlin, 1961. *John Heartfield: Leben und Werk*. Dresden, 1971. In Paul Raabe, *The Era of German Expressionism*. London, 1980. In Lucy Lippard, *Dadas on Art*. Englewood Cliffs, 1971.

[4] Egon Erwin Kisch, *Sensation Fair*. New York, 1941.

[5] Ernst Blass, "The Old Cafe des Westens"; in Raabe.

[6] John Willet, *Expressionism*. New York, 1970.

[7] Herzfelde

[8] "To the Civilized World: The Manifesto of the German University Professors and Men of Science," in R. H. Lutz, *The Fall of the German Empire*, Vol. 1. Palo Alto, 1932.

[9] Herzfelde

[10] Richard Huelsenbeck in Robert Motherwell, *Dada Painters and Poets*. New York, 1951.

[11] Walter Benjamin, "Theories of German Fascism", *New German Critique*, No. 17, 1979.

[12] Cited in John Laffin, *Letters from the Front*. London, 1973.

[13] Herzfelde

[14] Karl Liebknecht, *Militarism and Anti-Militarism*. New York, 1972.

[15] Erwin Piscator, *The Political Theater*. New York, 1978.

[16] Herzfelde

[17] Herzfelde

[18] Herzfelde

[19] Kisch, ibid.

[20] Grosz in Piscator, ibid.

[21] Herzfelde

[22] Herzfelde

[23] Cited in Raabe.

[24] Cited in Hans Hess, *George Grosz*. New York, 1974.

[25] Herzfelde

[26] Hans J. Kleinschmidt, "Berlin Dada" in Stephen Foster and Rudolf Kuenzli, *Dada Spectrum: The Dialectics of Revolt*. Madison, 1979.

[27] Harry Kessler, *Tagebücher*. Frankfurt, 1962. Also, *In the Twenties*. London, 1971.

[28] Walter Mehring, *Berlin Dada*. Zurich, 1959.

[29] Rosa Leviné-Meyer, *Leviné: The Life of a Revolutionary*. Glasgow, 1973.

[30] Eckhard Siepmann, *Montage: John Heartfield*. Berlin, 1977.

[31] Babette Gross, *Willi Münzenberg: A Political Biography*. Michigan State Univ., 1974.

[32] Beth Irwin Lewis, *George Grosz: Art and Politics in the Weimar Republic*. Madison, 1971.

[33] Herzfelde

[34] Walter Benjamin, "The Author as Producer" in *Reflections*. New York, 1978.

[35] Piscator, ibid. Also Maria Ley-Piscator, *The Piscator Experiment*. New York, 1967. C. D. Innes, *Erwin Piscator's Political Theatre*. London, 1972. John Willet, *The Theatre of Erwin Piscator*. London, 1978.

[36] Piscator, ibid.

[37] John Heartfield, "Daumier im Reich" in Siepmann, ibid. Also, Walter Benjamin, "Eduard Fuchs: Collector and Historian" in Andrew Arato and Eike Gebhardt, *The Essential Frankfurt School Reader*. New York, 1978.

[38] Henry James, *Daumier—Caricurist*. Emmaus, Pennsylvania, 1954.

[39] Josep Renau, "Homage to Heartfield", *PhotoVision 1*. Madrid, July-August 1981. Also cited in Peter K. Klein, "Art and Revolution in the Spanish Civil War (1936-1939), *Proceedings of the Caucus for Marxism and Art at the College Art Association Convention*, January 1978.

[40] Helmut Gruber, "Willi Münzenberg's German Communist Propaganda Empire, 1921-1933", *Journal of Modern History*, No. 38, September 1966. Also Babette Gross, ibid.

[41] Istvan Deak, *Weimar Germany's Left-Wing Intellectuals: A Political History of the Weltbühne and Its Circle*. Berkeley, 1968. Also Kurt Tucholsky, *Deutschland, Deutschland über alles*. Amherst, 1972 and Berlin, 1929; "Die Tendenzfotografie" (1925), *Gesammelte Werke, Band II 1925-1928*. Hamburg, 1964.

[42] Gross, ibid.

[43] Mehring, ibid.

[44] Walter Benjamin, "One-Way Street", *Reflections*. New York, 1978.

[45] Siepmann, ibid.

[46] Franz Neumann, *Behemoth: The Structure and Practice of National Socialism, 1933-44*. New York, 1944.

[47] Neumann, ibid.

[48] Richard Hunt, *German Social Democracy 1918-1933*. New Haven, 1964. Erich Matthias, "The Downfall of the Old Social Democratic Party in 1933", in Hajo Holborn, *Republic to Reich*. New York, 1972.

[49] Arthur Koestler, *Bricks to Babel*. New York, 1980.

[50] Siepmann, ibid.

[51] Wilhelm Reich, "What is Class Consciousness?" in Lee Baxandall, ed., *Sex-Pol*. New York, 1972. Also, *People in Trouble*. New York, 1976 and *Mass Psychology of Fascism*. New York, 1970.

[52] Ernst Fischer, *An Opposing Man*. New York, 1974 or *Erinnerung und Reflexionen*. Hamburg, 1969.

[53] Simone Pétrement, *Simone Weil: A Life*. New York, 1976.

[54] Siegfried Kracauer, *From Caligari to Hitler*. Princeton, 1947.

[55] Sergei Eisenstein, *Film Form*. New York, 1949.

[56] Cited in Herzfelde, *John Heartfield: Leben und Werk*. Also, George Lukacs, "Realism in the Balance," in Ernst Bloch, et. al., *Aesthetics and Politics*. London, 1977.

[57] André Breton, "Interview with *Indice*", in Franklin Rosemont, ed., *What is Surrealism?* New York, 1978.

[58] Gershom Scholem, *Major Trends in Jewish Mysticism*. New York, 1941.

[59] For compilation films: Robert C. Williams, *Artists in Revolution: Portraits of the Russian Avant-garde, 1905-1925*. Bloomington, 1977. Jay Leyda, *Kino*. New York, 1970. Joris Ivens, *The Camera and I*. Berlin, 1969. Bert Hogenkamp, "Workers' Newsreels in the Netherlands (1930-1931)," in Armand Mattelart and Seth Siegelaub, eds., *Communication and Class Struggle: Vol. 2. Liberation, Socialism*. New York, 1983. Béla Balás, "Build an International Union of Revolutionary Cinema," *Millenium Film Journal*, Nos. 4/5, Summer/Fall 1979. Kracauer, ibid. Piscator, ibid.

[60] Gustav Regler, *The Owl of Minerva*, New York, 1960.

[61] Regler, ibid.

[62] Yves Aubry, "Marinus Jacob Kjelgaard." *Zoom* (French ed.), January/February, 1978.

[63] Klaus Staeck, catalogue statement, *Art into Society—Society into Art*. ICA, London, 1974.

[64] Hans Haacke, "Where the Consciousness Industry is Concentrated," an interview with Catherine Lord in Douglas Kahn and Diane Neumaier, eds., *Cultures in Contention*. Seattle, 1985.

[65] Douglas Kahn, interview with SSS, *Spar* (Seattle), January 1982.

[66] Peter King, "The Art of Billboard Utilizing," in Kahn and Neumaier, ibid.

[67] Günter Wallraff, "The Coup Merchants," *The Undesirable Journalist*. Woodstock, 1979. Also, reprinted in Kahn and Neumaier, ibid. and Albert Camigliano, "The Portugese Revolution and the German Connection (Merci but no coup): An Introduction to Wallraff," in Kahn and Neumaier.

[68] "Tapes Mock Polish Government," Associated Press wire copy, *San Francisco Chronicle*, 19 December 1983.

[69] Paul Krassner, *How a Satirical Editor Became a Yippie Conspirator in Ten Easy Years*. New York, 1971 and *Best of the Realist*. Philadelphia, 1984.

[70] Ken Knabb, ed., *Situationist International Anthology*. Berkeley, 1981.

[71] Tom Ward, "The Situationists Reconsidered," in Kahn and Neumaier, ibid.

[72] Dziga Vertov, "The Vertov Papers," in Theresa Hak Kyung Cha, ed., *Apparatus*. New York, 1980.

[73] Roland Barthes, "The Photographic Message." *Image-Music-Text*. New York, 1977.

PHOTO CREDITS